TRACING YOUR CHANNEL ISLANDS ANCESTORS

FAMILY HISTORY FROM PEN & SWORD

Tracing Your Yorkshire Ancestors
Rachel Bellerby

Tracing Your Royal Marine Ancestors
Richard Brooks and Matthew Little

Tracing Your Pauper Ancestors
Robert Burlison

Tracing Your Labour Movement Ancestors
Mark Crail

Tracing Your Army Ancestors
Simon Fowler

A Guide to Military History on the Internet
Simon Fowler

Tracing Your Northern Ancestors
Keith Gregson

Your Irish Ancestors
Ian Maxwell

Tracing Your Scottish Ancestors
Ian Maxwell

Tracing Your London Ancestors
Jonathan Oates

Tracing Your Air Force Ancestors
Phil Tomaselli

Tracing Your Secret Service Ancestors
Phil Tomaselli

Tracing Your Criminal Ancestors
Stephen Wade

Tracing Your Police Ancestors
Stephen Wade

Tracing Your Jewish Ancestors
Rosemary Wenzerul

Fishing and Fishermen
Martin Wilcox

TRACING YOUR CHANNEL ISLANDS ANCESTORS

A Guide for Family Historians

Marie-Louise Backhurst

Pen & Sword
FAMILY HISTORY

First published in Great Britain in 2011 by
PEN & SWORD FAMILY HISTORY
an imprint of
Pen & Sword Books Ltd
47 Church Street
Barnsley
South Yorkshire
S70 2AS

Copyright © Marie-Louise Backhurst 2011

ISBN 978 1 84884 372 1

The right of Marie-Louise Backhurst to be identified as Author of this Work has been asserted by her in accordance with the Copyright, Designs and Patents Act 1988.

A CIP catalogue record for this book is available from the British Library.

All rights reserved. No part of this book may be reproduced or transmitted in any form or by any means, electronic or mechanical including photocopying, recording or by any information storage and retrieval system, without permission from the Publisher in writing.

Typeset in Palatino and Optima by
Phoenix Typesetting, Auldgirth, Dumfriesshire

Printed and bound in England by
CPI UK

Pen & Sword Books Ltd incorporates the imprints of
Pen & Sword Aviation, Pen & Sword Maritime, Pen & Sword Military, Wharncliffe Local History, Pen and Sword Select, Pen and Sword Military Classics, Leo Cooper, Remember When, Seaforth Publishing and Frontline Publishing.

For a complete list of Pen & Sword titles please contact
PEN & SWORD BOOKS LIMITED
47 Church Street, Barnsley, South Yorkshire, S70 2AS, England
E-mail: enquiries@pen-and-sword.co.uk
Website: www.pen-and-sword.co.uk

CONTENTS

Introduction		1

Part One: Internet Resources and Sources Outside the Islands
Chapter 1	Internet Resources	7
Chapter 2	Sources Outside the Islands	12

Part Two: Jersey
Chapter 3	General Description of the Geography, History and Administration	15
Chapter 4	Civil Records and Censuses	19
Chapter 5	Church Registers, Names and Cemeteries	28
Chapter 6	Property and Official Records	46
Chapter 7	Education, Employment and Crime	57
Chapter 8	Military and Migration	67

Part Three: Guernsey, Herm and Jethou
Chapter 9	General Description of the Geography, History and Administration	77
Chapter 10	Civil Records and Censuses	83
Chapter 11	Church Registers, Names and Cemeteries	90
Chapter 12	Property and Official Records	98
Chapter 13	Education, Employment and Crime	102
Chapter 14	Military and Migration	109

Part Four: Alderney

Chapter 15	General Description of the Geography, History and Administration	115
Chapter 16	Civil Records and Censuses	119
Chapter 17	Church Registers, Names and Cemeteries	122
Chapter 18	Property and Official Records	127
Chapter 19	Education, Employment and Crime	130
Chapter 20	Military and Migration	132

Part Five: Sark

Chapter 21	General Description of the Geography, History and Administration	137
Chapter 22	Civil Records and Censuses	141
Chapter 23	Church Registers, Names and Cemeteries	142
Chapter 24	Property and Official Records	146
Chapter 25	Education, Employment and Crime	148
Chapter 26	Military and Migration	151

Useful Local Records and Private Archives	153
Directory of Family History Societies, Libraries and Archives	157
Directory of Places of Historic Interest to Visit	167
Glossary	169
Select Bibliography	175
Index	179

For Michael,
for his complete lack of interest in family history

ACKNOWLEDGEMENTS

I am grateful for the assistance of many islanders, in particular: in Jersey, Virginia Gruchy, Alex Glendinning, Mary Billot, David Le Maistre, Robert Kerley, former Superintendent Registrar, Sue Groves, Superintendent Registrar, Anna Baghiani of the Lord Coutanche Library, Société Jersiaise, Linda Romeril and the staff of the Jersey Archive; in Guernsey, Marie Sillars, Juliette Hargieton and Maria van der Tang, of the Family History Section, La Société Guernesiaise, Amanda Bennett of the Priaulx Library, Ken Tough, Her Majesty's Greffier and Dr Darryl Ogier and staff, Island Archives, and Gillian Lenfenstey; in Alderney, Eileen Mignot and Alexandra Gordon-Jones of the Alderney Museum; in Sark, Richard Axton and Anthony Dunks; and many of the members of the Channel Islands Family History Society who have helped over the years.

All the photographs and the maps are from the author's own collection; all postcards are from a private collection with kind permission. The photographs of the Alderney land-distribution map and register of evacuees are reproduced with the permission of the Alderney Society Museum.

INTRODUCTION

The Channel Islands are a group of seven inhabited islands, and several uninhabited ones, situated in the Bay of Mont St Michel, between the French provinces of Normandy and Brittany.

The inhabited islands are Jersey, Guernsey, Herm, Jethou, Alderney, Sark and Brecqhou. They have a very long and distinctive history, which is, perhaps, little known. Yet the names of Jersey, Guernsey and Alderney are synonymous throughout the world with knitted goods and cattle. Although geographically adjacent to France, they have been possessions of the English Crown since 1204 and are consequently known as Crown Dependencies. They have very strong ties to Great Britain, but are not a part of it or of the United Kingdom. Together with the Isle of Man, they comprise the 'Islands in the British Seas'. They do not belong to the European Union, but have associate membership.

Of enormous military and strategic value to the United Kingdom, the islands have been heavily fortified throughout the centuries. The islands were invaded many times by the French, the Spaniards and, in the twentieth century, by the Germans.

The Channel Islands are self-governing and many of their laws are Norman French in origin. Until the middle of the twentieth century, French was the official language and many surnames and place names are also French in origin. Islanders spoke their own languages – Jèrriais, Dgèrnésiais (or Guernésiais), Auriginais and Sercquiais – but the written records were kept in French.

Inevitably in such small islands intermarriage between cousins was common and the small number of surnames can make for very confusing family trees. There were, however, sufficiently large populations in most of the islands and migration helped to widen the gene pool. Immigrants have come from all over the world, but particularly from England and France. Many immigrants stayed a few years in one island and then moved to another, so research in several of the islands may be necessary.

The Calvinist ministers who came to the islands from the sixteenth century onwards narrowly limited the Christian names that could be chosen, so identifying the correct Jean (John) Le Gresley, for example, can be nearly impossible. It is only by using a wide variety of sources that such identifications can be verified properly. This book shows the many different sources that, taken together, can make up the whole picture. Using these sources can also build not just a family tree, but a real family history, giving a feel for the

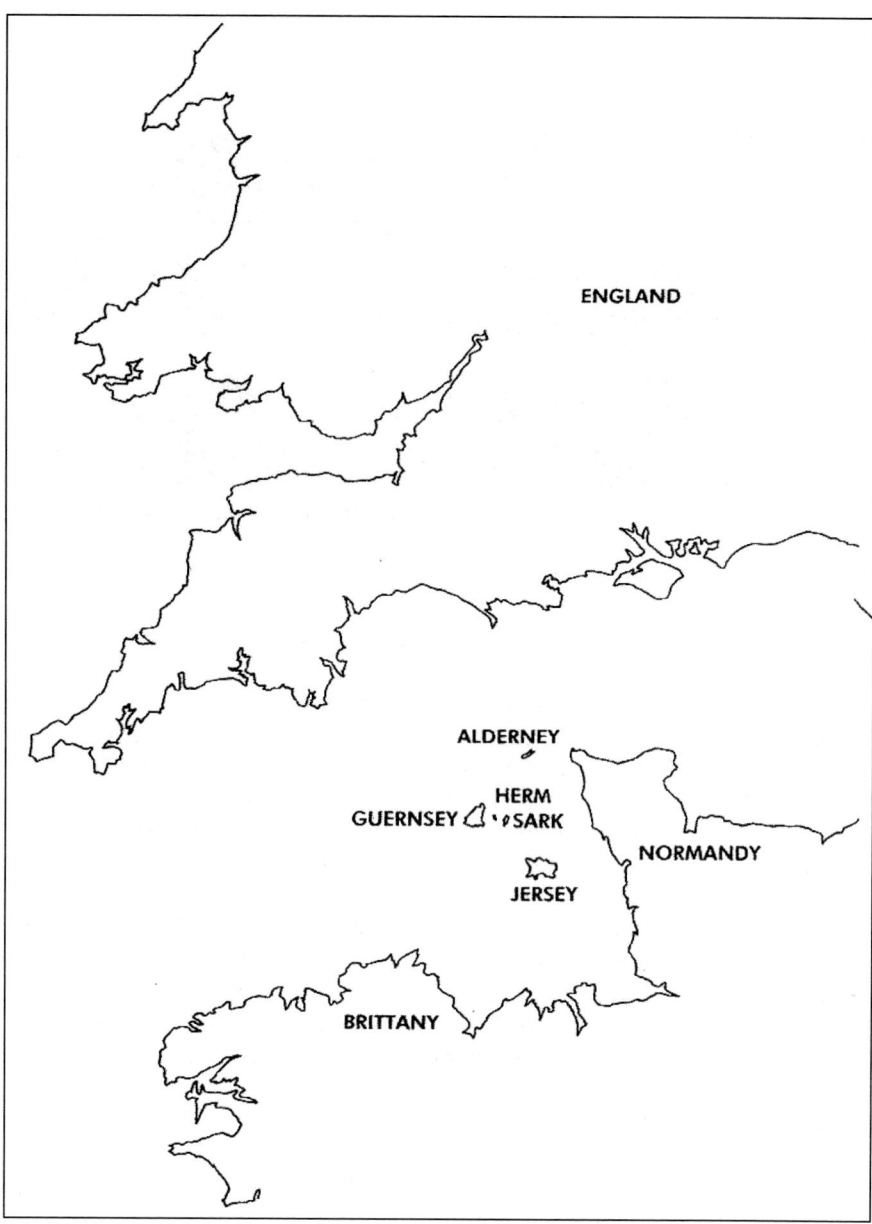

Map of the Channel Islands, showing their position in relation to France and England

View from St Peter Port, Guernsey, showing Castle Cornet with (from the left) the islands of Herm, Jethou and Sark in the distance

lives that your ancestors would have led on the beautiful, but challenging, Channel Islands.

As in England, the Gregorian calendar came into force in the islands in September 1752, so the dating system is identical to England – and the first day of the year was moved from 25 March to 1 January thereafter.

Although many of the genealogical records in the Channel Islands are similar to those in England, there are notable differences, both between the islands and the mainland (which is what locals call England – not France) and between the islands themselves. This book is intended as a summary of these differences. Many records of the history of your family and the community in the Channel Islands were previously unavailable to the general public but are now readily accessible, so tracing your family's history can now be much more than simply gathering names. However, the vast majority of the records for researching your Channel Islands family history are available only in the islands and copies are not kept in the United Kingdom or elsewhere.

This book has been written to assist you with your research into your Channel Islands family history, whether you live in the islands or elsewhere. There are a number of sources that can be consulted from outside the islands but, if you are unable to visit and wish to engage the services of a researcher, do remember to give all the information you currently have, making it quite clear what you want the researcher to find for you. Try to make your enquiry as succinct as possible; there are many different organisations that can assist you, but it is better to confine yourself to one at a time.

It is quite possible that your family tree has already been traced, so although the information should always be double-checked, it is worth

First Tower railway station, St Hellier, Jersey, built about 1871. The Jersey Railway Company was established in 1870 and linked the town of St Helier with the town of St Aubin to the west. The tower was built in about 1782 to defend the island against attack by the French.

finding out from the societies/libraries/archives in the islands (addresses can be found in the Directory at the back of the book) if a tree already exists.

If you are travelling to the islands, do inform the societies, libraries and archives of your visit as they can prepare material and let you know if there are any closures during your time in the islands. Remember that travel to the islands can be subject to delays due to weather (and even ash from a volcano, as happened to the author), so plan your visit accordingly. The tourism offices in each island can assist with travel arrangements and accommodation.

Administratively, the islands consist of the Bailiwicks of Jersey and Guernsey, and this book deals with each island separately, as the records are different and are kept in different ways. Although the Bailiwick of Guernsey includes Alderney, Sark, Herm and Jethou, there are separate records for the two larger islands. Some of the general comments made in the Jersey and Guernsey sections concerning parish registers will, in the main, apply to all the islands.

The information in this book is as comprehensive and up-to-date as possible, but the author fully recognises that there will be omissions as well as mistakes, so will be grateful for any corrections. These will be put on the website of the Channel Islands Family History Society: www.jerseyfamily history.org.

PART ONE

Internet Resources and Sources Outside the Islands

Chapter 1

INTERNET RESOURCES

During the last ten years an enormous quantity of genealogical records and family trees have been made available through the Internet. Most official records in the Channel Islands, however, have not yet been digitised, so cannot be accessed in this way.

There are, though, a number of websites that are useful to those tracing their Channel Islands ancestry. Their usefulness is varied as some are not updated regularly and some links no longer work. Inevitably, websites change and information will become out of date, so double-checking may be necessary. As the information in this book will also be superseded, your first port of call should be to the Channel Islands Family History Society (CIFHS) website (www.jerseyfamilyhistory.org), which will lead you to all the updated information and links. The society's website also has contents of its own journal, information on the society's research group and publications available to purchase.

The websites listed below are those that are well known, but there may well be others that the author has not yet discovered.

Cyndi's List (www.cyndislist.com) is a well-known portal that is regularly updated, and the information on the Channel Islands is at: www.cyndislist.com/channel.htm.

The GENUKI website (www.genuki.org.uk) has a page on the Channel Islands, but much of it is now out of date (it was last updated in 2001), most of the links do not work and the email address is no longer valid. However, some of the pages have been archived on: http://user.itl.net/~glen/CIintro.html or see: http://user.itl.net/~glen/genukici.html and then look at each individual island. These pages give some useful information, such as a page of historical descriptions of the Channel Islands from Grose's *The Antiquities of England and Wales*, published in 1777, which is at: http://user.itl.net/~glen/description.html.

For general information on Jersey genealogy and much else, including photographs of churches, see Geoff Wright's Genealogy Pages at: www.avoncliffe.com/genealogy/jersey/ci-index.htm.

The Channel Islands Webring (http://w.webring.com/hub?ring=chigen-ring) gives links to the websites of several family histories – such as the Carey family at www.careyroots.com, the Poindexter Family Association at www.poindexterfamily.org and Tony and Angela Bellows's site at:

http://members.societe-jersiaise.org/whitsco/, which includes information from families from Jersey and Guernsey and also gives a lot of information on other matters of interest to family historians.

Started in 2010 Donkipedia (www.guernsey-society.org.uk/donkipedia/) and Jerripedia (www.guernsey-society.org.uk/donkipedia/index.php5?title=Jerripedia) both give an increasing amount of information on the history of the islands and family trees. Both sites encourage researchers to add to the information.

Family Tree Forum (www.familytreeforum.com/content.php/300-Channel-Islands) has a page on the Channel Islands that includes links, but some are now out of date.

The Church of Jesus Christ of the Latter-Day Saints (LDS), although based in Salt Lake City, has centres all over the world. Although there are some Channel Island families (particularly Guernsey civil registers) on their website (www.familysearch.org), the majority of the information comes from members, so will need double-checking. The parish registers, however, have not been microfilmed. Available to order from the centres are microfilm records, such as the indexes to the Guernsey civil registration records from 1840, wills of personalty and Royal Court records up to 1900, and in Jersey: land records, the *Registre Public*, and records of the Royal Court. It is likely that these may be digitised in the near future. There is also some genealogical information on their website: https://wiki.familysearch.org/en/Guernsey or https://wiki.familysearch.org/en/Jersey but some of the information is now outdated. They also have a library with books on the Channel Islands.

The Channel Islands Mailing List (http://lists.rootsweb.ancestry.com/index/intl/UK/CHANNEL-ISLANDS.html) is a useful means of contacting fellow researchers, many of whom not only exchange information but are also prepared to do 'look-ups'. The website gives full instructions on how to subscribe and there is an archive.

There is a surname list that was hosted by the late John Fuller on Rootsweb (www.rootsweb.ancestry.com/~jfuller/ci/surnames.txt), which is now updated at: www.rootsweb.ancestry.com/~ukchanis/. For information on surnames see: http://freepages.genealogy.rootsweb.ancestry.com/~egreef/channelislandsurnames.htm.

Each of the large genealogical websites have Channel Islands message boards – those for Rootsweb/Ancestry are at http://boards.rootsweb.com/localities.britisles.channelislands.general/mb.ashx or at http://boards.ancestry.com/localities.britisles.channelislands/mb.ashx. The GenForum message board at http://genforum.com does not give separate boards for the Channel Islands, but it may be worthwhile looking under individual names, including Jersey, Guernsey, Alderney and Sark. The Rootschat Forum, which is at www.rootschat.com, includes a page for the Channel Islands.

All the major subscribing genealogical websites include the Channel

Islands. The censuses for 1841, 1851, 1861, 1871, 1891 and 1901 and some indexes are also available on CDs from S&N Genealogy Supplies (www.genealogysupplies.com). They also offer CDs of *Kelly's Directory for the Channel Islands* for 1923 and the *Homeland Handbooks* for 1933 (except for Jersey), which include maps.

For free census indexes see Lorna Pratt's website (www.members.shaw.ca/jerseymaid/), which covers all the islands for 1841, although not complete. The 1881 census for the Channel Islands is freely available at www.familysearch.org.

There are many references to the Channel Islands and to individuals from the islands on the website of The National Archives (www.nationalarchives.gov.uk/) and through it you can access the county records offices, society archives and other archives held throughout England and Wales: www.nationalarchives.gov.uk/a2a/ ('Access to Archives', A2A). For example, wills of soldiers appear on The National Archives and resettlement examinations appear on A2A, particularly in county records that are close to the islands. The library at The National Archives in Kew also has a good selection of books, and has, for example, a number of bulletins of the Société Jersiaise, books on all the islands and a *Kelly's Directory* for 1939. Their catalogue is online at: www.library.nationalarchives.gov.uk/.

The Archon Directory on The National Archives site (www.nationalarchives.gov.uk/archon/searches/locresult.asp?lctry=Channel%20Islands) gives a list of record repositories in the Channel Islands with links to websites, including archives, record offices, museums and libraries.

The commercial genealogical websites include the ability to put family trees onto them and these can then be searched for Channel Island names. If you do a general search do not forget that the word 'Jersey' often appears under New Jersey or the Earl of Jersey, and St Helier may refer to the hospital of that name in Carshalton, Surrey. So it is best to use, for example, 'NOT New' in the search box, to exclude those references to New Jersey.

The *Oxford Dictionary of National Biography* has entries on several Channel Islanders and is available in public libraries, and online through public library membership, at: www.oxforddnb.com.

For information on the First World War and the Channel Islands see the Great War Study Group at: www.greatwarci.net. There is an interesting contributory website on the Jersey Pals at: www.jerseypals.com.

The Channel Islands Occupation Society has a great deal of material on the German Occupation of the islands during the Second World War; there are two groups, one for Jersey: www.ciosjersey.org.uk and the other for the Bailiwick of Guernsey: www.occupied.guernsey.net.

The following websites are of general interest to those searching for Channel Islands ancestors; more specific websites are mentioned throughout the text or in the Directory of Societies, Archives and Libraries.

For all these islands see the entries on Wikipedia or in encyclopedias. See also: www.britlink.org/channel.html.

Jersey

The Société Jersiaise (www.societe-jersiaise.org) has a page on family history research. On its members' page there is a discussion forum that includes queries about family history.

The Jersey Archive has several helpful pages on subjects such as: family history and house history at: www.jerseyheritage.org/research-centre /information-leaflets. Their catalogue (www.jerseyheritagetrust.jeron.je/) allows searches on archaeology, archives, art, museum objects, register of documents held elsewhere, natural history and the historic buildings register. The most helpful list for family historians is of the post-1842 baptisms for St Helier and the registration cards created during the German Occupation (1940–45). See below for further information.

The *Jersey Evening Post* has a page called 'Jersey Connections' that includes news and enquiries on family history: www.thisisjersey.com/section/ jersey-connections/keep-in-touch/.

For modern telephone directories see: www.jerseyinsight.com/directory. Channel Islands electoral lists are not online. For general information on Jersey see: www.jersey.com and www.gov.je/.

Guernsey

The Priaulx Library website (www.priaulxlibrary.co.uk/priaulx-library-services-research.asp) gives information on family history research. For researchers with roots in Guernsey, surname databases containing many local names and references for a few cemeteries, including an index for the Strangers' Cemetery, there is a general site on: www.genealogy .guernsey.net.

'This is Guernsey Forum' offers users the opportunity to read letters that have appeared in the *Guernsey Press and Star*, and a place to search for old friends and relatives and to reminisce about life in the island: www.thisis guernsey.co.uk/discus/messages/53/53.html.

For modern telephone directories see: www.theguernseydirectory.com/. For general information on Guernsey see: www.gov.gg/ccm/navigation/ about-guernsey/ and www.visitguernsey.com/; www.heritageguernsey .com/has a page about family history in the island and information on the history generally.

Herm and Jethou

For general information see: www.herm.com. The Faed family lived in Jethou 1964–71 and more information can be found on: www.faed.net/ cfaed/jethou/jethou.htm.

Alderney

Peter Hamer's website gives a lot of information on family and local history, including transcripts of the censuses: http://sites.google.com/site/alderneylocalhistory/Home. For general information see: www.alderney.gov.gg and: http://visitalderney.com/.

Sark

For information on the archival holdings of the Société Serquaise see: www.socsercq.sark.gg/archives.html. There is also material on Sark in the Priaulx Library and the Island Archives in Guernsey (see Directory). For general information see: www.gov.sark.gg, www.welcometosark.com, www.simplysark.info and www.sark.info.

Chapter 2

SOURCES OUTSIDE THE ISLANDS

The Society of Genealogists has a good collection of material on the Channel Islands, including the microfilms of Guernsey civil registration. Further details of their holdings are on: www.sog.org.uk/prc/channelislands.shtml. Members can borrow books.

As well as using the online catalogues of the local libraries (see Directory below) inter-library loans are possible with all of them. There is a good bibliography on Jersey by Richard Hemery at: http://jerseyfamilyhistory.co.uk. Vince Gardiner also published a book on the Channel Islands in the World Bibliographical Series, see: www.angelfire.com/biz6/vghome/THECHANNEL ISLANDSBIBLIOG.htm.

Many older Channel Island books have now been digitised by Google Books, including *An Armorial of Jersey* by James B. Payne, *The History of Guernsey* by Jonathan Duncan and *The Alderney Guide* by Louisa Lane Clarke.

Some Channel Island newspapers are held at the British Library at Colindale; their catalogue is www.bl.uk and some of these newspapers may be digitised. The British Library also has a collection of Channel Islands books and maps. A useful almanac is that of *Robson's Guernsey and Jersey Directory* for 1839, which has been digitised on the Ancestry website (http://search.ancestry.co.uk/Browse/view.aspx?dbid=1547&iid=GB1324-00000). Although the Channel Islands are not mentioned on the www.historicaldirectories.org website, a search on the names of the islands does bring up some references.

PART TWO

Jersey

Chapter 3

GENERAL DESCRIPTION OF THE GEOGRAPHY, HISTORY AND ADMINISTRATION

The Bailiwick of Jersey contains the largest Channel Island, measuring about nine miles by five, with steep cliffs to the north and sandy beaches in the south and west. It is about twelve miles from Normandy, and about eighty miles from the south coast of England.

The principal town of Jersey is St Helier; there is a small town in the south, St Aubin, and a village in the east, Gorey. There are twelve parishes, namely: St Helier, St Lawrence, St Saviour, Grouville, St Martin, St Clement, St John, Trinity, St Mary, St Brelade, St Peter and St Ouen. They are both ecclesiastical and civil parishes. The Constable (*Connétable*) is the elected head of the civil parish and has *Centeniers* and *Vingteniers* (see Glossary) to assist in policing; there are also *Procureurs du Bien Publique* who attend to the finances. The Royal Court makes a visit to each parish every six years (*La Visite Royale*) to check the finances, the roads and any other matters.

The Church of England is the established Church in the Island. Originally a part of the Diocese of Coutances in Normandy, the island became a part of the Diocese of Winchester in 1499, although this did not take effect until 1568. The Dean of Jersey, a non-voting member of the States of Jersey, is appointed by the Crown from one of the twelve parish rectors. They take an active part in the administrative life of the parish as well as the ecclesiastical.

The local parliament is known as the States, as it was originally composed of the three *États* (States), namely, the Jurats (judiciary), the rectors (church) and the Constables (the civil administrators of the parishes). Today all members of the States are elected as Senators, Deputies or Constables. The Crown is represented by a Lieutenant Governor.

The Bailiff is the highest appointed Crown officer of the Royal Court and President of the States. There are various other States and Royal Court officials, some of whose records are useful to family historians.

The population of Jersey has always been relatively high for the small size of the island. At the end of the seventeenth century immigration to the American colonies was recommended by the States. By the eighteenth century the population was just under 20,000; this was increased by French

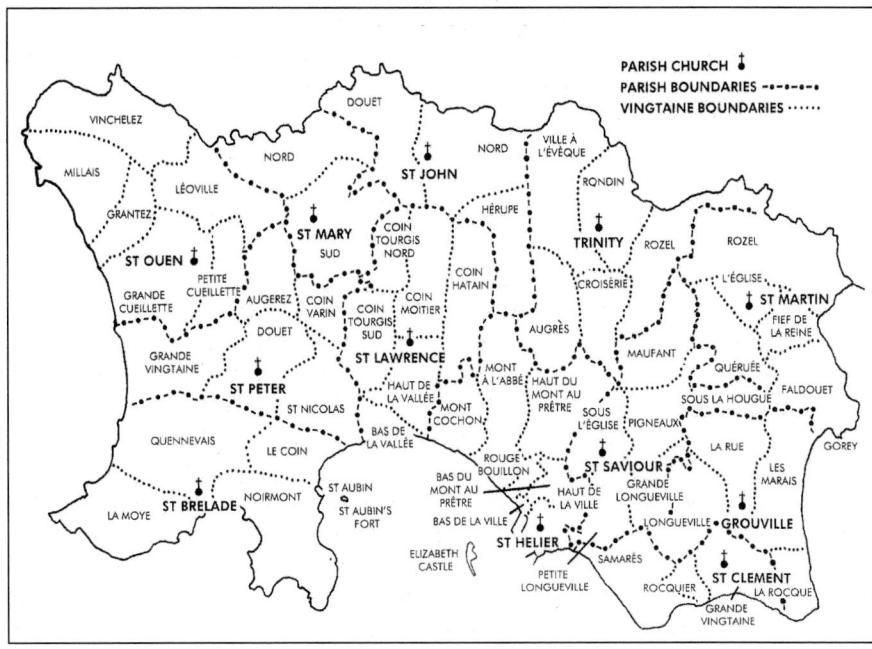

Map of the island of Jersey, showing parish and vingtaine boundaries

immigrants and the English garrison. The nineteenth century saw an explosion in the population and by the 1851 census it had increased to 57,020. Stagnation then set in and the next spurt of growth was not until after the Second World War; by the early 1960s the population had reached 63,550 and, according to the census taken in 1991, it stood at 84,082. The latest estimated figure is 92,000.

A quarter of a million years ago Neanderthal man lived in what is now a cave in St Brelade. Jersey was then part of the European landmass and did not become an island until about 4,000 BC when it was inhabited by Neolithic people; their monuments, such as dolmens, are scattered throughout the island.

There is little evidence of extensive Roman settlement, although the island may have been used as a strategic outpost. Vikings attacked the island and may also have settled – many of the coastal place names are of Viking origin. The island came under the jurisdiction of the Norman duchy and a feudal system of *seigneurs* and their tenants was established. After the loss of Normandy by King John in 1204, Jersey came under the English Crown. The island probably then enjoyed a period of prosperity, although it was attacked by the French and Spanish on many occasions. The Black Death in 1348 probably resulted in the death of half the population; it is believed that the plague was carried to England by vessels from the Channel Islands.

Before the Reformation Jersey was a Catholic island with an abbey and several priories. A strong Calvinist tradition was established after the Reformation dating from the early French Huguenot refugees who came to the island in the sixteenth and seventeenth centuries. As a French-speaking island, the ministers came from France, Switzerland or Italy where Calvinism predominated. In the late eighteenth century, Methodism came to the island via Newfoundland and, although initially resisted, became a strong force. The majority of islanders, however, belong to the Church of England, which has twelve parish churches and several other churches, particularly in St Helier. From the time of the French Revolution in the late eighteenth century, a small Roman Catholic community was established and eventually several chapels were built. Catholicism has grown in strength mainly because of immigration of the French, Irish, Italian, Portuguese and Polish people who have settled in the island over the last 200 years.

Throughout the centuries the island has acted as a place of refuge, particularly for French religious and political refugees and British taxpayers. Equally, many islanders have emigrated to many different countries, especially Canada, America, Australia and New Zealand.

The island is very fertile and agriculture plays an important part in island life. The Jersey cow and the Jersey Royal potato are both well known around the world. The present economy is heavily dependent on the finance industry. Tourism, which began in the middle of the nineteenth century, brings visitors from all over the world. In the past, the cod fisheries off Newfoundland, privateering and smuggling all brought riches to the island, still visible in the many fine Jersey houses, some of which are still known as 'cod houses'.

Jersey was always in danger of attack from the French, and was occupied by them for several years in the fifteenth century. One of the last battles

St Lawrence Parish Hall, Jersey, built in 1882. Uniquely, the parish church, parish hall and parish school are all in a continuous line along the main road.

fought on British soil took place in 1781 when a French adventurer, Baron de Rullecourt, landed on the island and demanded that the Governor surrender. Fortunately, the British troops stationed in the island and the local militia came to the rescue and fought a pitched battle in the Royal Square. The French were defeated and their leader killed, although so too was the British commander, Major Peirson. In consequence of this, and the subsequent threats posed by Napoleon, the island was heavily fortified. During the Second World War the island was occupied by the Germans for five years, and many of their fortifications, built mostly by slave labour, are still highly visible today.

After the invasion of France, it rapidly became evident that the Channel Islands could not be defended without loss of civilian life, and after a bombardment of St Helier resulting in nine deaths, the island surrendered to the Germans on 1 July 1940. Privations followed, with imprisonment and deportations for many islanders. Liberation finally came on 9 May 1945. After the German Occupation the island developed a very successful tourist industry, and since the 1960s the financial services industry has grown in strength.

Although the language in most common use was Jèrriais (Jersey Norman French), islanders would also have been conversant in French, and virtually all the records up until 1948 are in French. However, English was widely spoken and increased in use during the nineteenth century. There are about 4,000 native speakers of Jèrriais in the island and courses are available for beginners.

Heraldry is a very specialised subject and the best source for information on heraldry in Jersey is a series of articles by Major N.V.L. Rybot in the annual bulletins of the Société Jersiaise for 1928 and 1929, and there is a forthcoming book, *The Heraldry of the Channel Islands*, by Guy Storey. James Bertrand Payne's *An Armorial of Jersey* also gives substantial information on local heraldry and the heraldry of families who married into island families, particularly those from Normandy. The family trees, however, although useful, are not always accurate. Few island families have had their coats of arms registered at the College of Arms – de Carteret being one notable exception. This was because the heralds' visitations did not include the Channel Islands; perhaps they felt the sea crossing would be too dangerous.

Chapter 4

CIVIL RECORDS AND CENSUSES

Civil Records

The civil registration of births, marriages and deaths started in Jersey in August 1842. In 2001 the Marriage and Civil Status Law came into effect, repealing all previous amendments. It would appear that registration was obligatory and fines could be made right from the introduction of the law, but this does not mean that all births were registered. Marriages and deaths, however, would have much higher coverage and missing records would be less common.

No copies of the Channel Island registers are kept by officials in England, nor are there are indexes on the Internet. The system comes under the control of the States of Jersey and the parishes; registers of births, non-Church of England marriages and deaths are kept by the registrar of each of the twelve parishes. The rectors of the twelve parish churches keep their own records. The registrars of St Helier are employed by the parish, but the other registrars act in an honorary position – they and the rectors make quarterly returns of their records to the Superintendent Registrar, whose office is in St Helier.

All enquiries for certificates and research should be directed to the Superintendent Registrar in St Helier (see Directory for full contact details). However, requests for certificates of births or deaths that took place in St Helier after 1999 should be addressed to: Register Office for the Parish of St Helier, 3 Vine Street, St Helier, Jersey JE2 4WB. There is access to the registers at the office of the Superintendent Registrar by appointment between 9 a.m. and 12.30 a.m., Monday to Friday. Ensure you telephone first as the office is also used for weddings. The indexes are at the front of each book, so searching can take some time.

Research charges can often be alleviated as the indexes to the Superintendent Registrar's copies 1842–1900 are available at the Société Jersiaise Library (SJL), the CIFHS research room at the Jersey Archive and at the Jersey Library.

Certificates were mostly in French, although sometimes if the family was English, then it might be in English. The information on the certificates is

EXTRACT FROM THE REGISTER OF MARRIAGES

ANNO DOMINI 1876

Of the Parish of **St. Helier**, in the Island of Jersey.

[PAGE 67]

Marriage solemnized in the Parish of **St. Helier**, in the Island of Jersey.

ANNO DOMINI 1876

No.	When Married.	Christian and Family Names of the Parties.	Age.	Condition.	Rank, Trade, or Profession.	Place of Residence at the time of Marriage.	Place of Birth.	Father's Name and Surname.	Rank, Trade, or Profession of the Father.
201	Twenty second day of March 1876	Clement de Gruchy	27	Bachelor	Cooper	No. 29 Parade	Pesier, France	Pierre de Gruchy	Wesleyan Minister
		Elizabeth Mill	28	Spinster	Bonnet Maker	Bath Street	Devonshire	Richard Mill	Saddler

Married in the Superintendent Registrar's Office by licence, John Borel, Superintendent Registrar.

This Marriage was solemnized between us { Clement de Gruchy / Elizabeth Mill }

In presence of { J. Naylor / Edwin Prout }

I hereby certify that the above is a true and faithful Extract from the Register of Marriages of the Parish of **St. Helier**, in the Island of Jersey.

Witness my hand, this **Eleventh** day of **March** 1979

Witnesses Henry J. Michel, Registrar

(SUPERINTENDENT Registrar)

A Jersey marriage certificate showing place of birth of the groom and bride different from that on certificates from England or Guernsey: in Jersey, marriage certificates give the place of birth of both the bride and groom.

On the birth certificate the following details are given: date and place of birth (usually the parish and *vingtaine*, though sometimes the address, particularly in St Helier); the time of birth in the case of a multiple birth; first name, if any (not compulsory); sex; name and first name of father; name and first name of mother; father's profession, occupation or status; signature, description and residence of informant; date of registration; signature of registrar; name at baptism if added later.

On the marriage certificate: date; parish; surnames and Christian names (baptised and family names) of the married couple; their age; condition, rank, status or profession; residence at time of marriage; place of birth; name and first name of father and his rank or profession; place where wedding took place; whether by banns, licence or special licence; by whom; signatures of the couple and witnesses.

On the death certificate: date and place of death; name and first name; sex; age; state or profession; cause of death; signature, description and place of residence of informant; date of registration.

The Superintendent Registrar has incomplete handwritten books compiled by the registrars of St Helier, which give the place of marriage of the parents of children born in the parish. These date from 1850 and are known as the *òu marier* (where married) books. If the date of birth is known, then this information can be supplied.

Births

Although civil registration was supposed to be comprehensive, in the early years some births escaped being registered. If a registered birth cannot be found in any of the parishes (and there is good reason to believe that your ancestor was born in the island) then it is quite possible that the person was baptised and that their baptism record would be in the Church registers. Occasionally a person will have given their place of birth as a certain parish on their marriage certificate, or on the census, and yet it cannot be found in that parish, in which case the neighbouring parishes should be searched, as it is quite likely that it could be found there.

Short birth certificates can also be issued but these are generally not very useful to researchers as they give only the date and place of birth.

Marriages

Illegitimate children were legitimised by the subsequent marriage of their parents and this is noted on the marriage certificate. For example, at the marriage of Peter Le Gresley and Jane Mary Simon in 1859, their son, Peter John, born 1858, was recognised. The wording may differ slightly, in this case it is stated that: *les parties ont présenté un enfant du nom de Peter John né le*

29 novembre 1858, et qu'ils ont reconnu et declare leur enfant naturel et habile à héritier (the parties have presented a child called Peter John born 29 November 1858, and they have recognised and declared him their natural child and capable of inheriting). Marriage registers are kept by the rectors for Church of England marriages and by the parish registrars for all other denominations, including civil marriages, so there are two separate books for each parish. The non-Anglican marriages date from the date of registration as a place for marriage, not the date of the opening of the church, so if a marriage is said to have taken place in, for example, St Mark prior to 1917 it would be registered in St Helier, rather than in the separate St Mark's book.

There are separate books for the additional Church of England churches in St Helier: All Saints 1872, St Simon 1872, St Andrew 1872, St Mark 1917 and St James 1904. St Paul, although belonging to the Church of England, is not a separate ecclesiastical district and so is included in the St Helier Church of England registers; its baptism records date from 1893. In St Saviour there is St Luke's Church built in 1852. Gouray Church registers date from 1901. St Aubin-on-the Hill in St Brelade, although consecrated in 1747, is not a separate district so marriages are recorded in the St Brelade's Church of England register. Similarly, marriages for St Matthew appear in the St Lawrence register and those for the church of St George (which was built in 1876) in St Ouen.

The non-Church of England registers for marriages start as follows: St Brelade 1870, St Clement 1846, Grouville 1901, St Helier 1842, St John 1848, St Lawrence 1869, St Martin 1854, St Mary 1923, St Ouen 1861, St Peter 1866, St Saviour 1872 and Trinity 1906.

Registry office weddings are conducted in the office of the Superintendent Registrar in Jersey since 1842, although with the introduction of the 2001 law marriages can also be conducted in different approved locations in the island – all these records are in the non-Anglican parish register.

Anglican marriages can be conducted after banns are read, a licence or a special licence given. Often a special licence was made to allow couples to be married at 6 a.m., which enabled them to catch the ferry for their honeymoon.

Quakers and Jews had a special provision for marriages: they did not require a parish registrar to be present, although they did need a licence from the Superintendent Registrar. All their marriage rites still have to be observed and the registrar of Quakers has to be notified; their records are kept separately. They could both register and license their own weddings, but this has changed with the Marriage and Civil Status Law (2001), which means that they need to obtain licences from the Superintendent Registrar and their premises have to be registered.

Deaths

Death certificates issued for those who die at sea in local waters are recorded in the St Helier registers. A register of stillbirths has been kept since 1961.

Certificates of births, marriages and deaths relating to Jersey people who were registered in England during the Second World War include their Jersey addresses in the occupation column; copies, which were sent to the island, are held by the Jersey Archive. Exceptionally, there are double registrations that are kept outside the island – these are for military families garrisoned in the island and for French nationals. (It may be possible that other nationalities can also register with their consul, either in the island or in England, but this has not been checked.) The regimental returns (also called chaplains' returns, army returns, etc.) for baptisms, births, marriages and deaths cover 1761 until 1924; marriages date from 1796. For further information see: www.wiki.fibis.org/index.php?title=Chaplains_Returns. The indexes for these are freely available on: www.familyrelatives.com and copies of the entries can be obtained from the General Register Office: www.gro.gov.uk/gro. There are also separate registers for births and deaths at sea, also available from the GRO, although those who died in local waters or those bodies which are washed ashore locally are registered in the St Helier deaths register.

French nationals registered births in Jersey with the French consul and these records are now kept in Nantes in the Archives Diplomatiques de France, Centre des Archives diplomatiques de Nantes (CADN) – www.diplomatie.gouv.fr/fr/ministere_817/archives-patrimoine_3512/archives-diplomatiques_5142/lieux-conservation_12634/nantes_12636/centre-archives-diplomatiques-nantes-cadn_27845.html – it is possible that nationals of other countries have also registered with their consul.

In Jersey an adoption register was begun in 1948. The records that the Children's Service has are more detailed from 1959 when the service was established. Anyone who was adopted and wishes to acquire a copy of their original birth certificate has to receive counselling. The counsellor will then write to the Superintendent Registrar requesting a copy of the original entry. Such counselling is provided by the Children's Services (address in Directory) and see: www.gov.je/Caring/Children/FosteringAdoption/Pages/AccessRecords.aspx.

There is a contact register for adopted persons and their birth relatives to record their wish for contact, which is managed by the Children's Service. The Service, along with the Children Board in Guernsey, keep records of any contact or request for information in their files and if they find that a contact from a birth parent matches with one from the adopted adult or vice versa, they will act as intermediary and put the two parties in touch with each other.

Censuses

Jersey was included in the census for England and Wales from 1821, but was not included in the two earlier counts of 1801 or 1811. The Channel Islands are included with the Isle of Man as Islands in the British Seas.

The first three censuses were destroyed after statistical analysis but the nominative returns survive from 1841 onwards. The returns are also subject to 100-year secrecy rules so the most recent census available is 1911.

The figures for Jersey were: in 1821 the population stood at 28,600; by 1831 it was 36,582; 1841, 47,544; 1851, 57,020; 1861, 55,613; 1871, 56,627; 1881, 52,445; 1891, 54,518; 1901, 52,276; 1911, 51,898; 1921, 49,701; 1931, 50,462 (burnt); 1940 (10 August), 41,101 (no names available, but see the registration cards); 1951, 57,310; 1961, 63,550; 1971, 69,329; 1981, 72,970; 1991, 84,082; and 2001, 87,186.

The 1841 census, taken on 6 June, is slightly different to the other censuses in that ages are given to the nearest five-year interval for all over the age of 15, so that everyone will be, for example, 20 or 35, but never 21 or 37. The place of birth is also not given in this census: in the birth column a 'yes' simply means born in the island, but 'no' may mean born in one of the other Channel Islands. In the next column letters indicate the place of birth – 'E' stands for England and Wales, 'S' for Scotland, 'I' for Ireland and 'F' for foreign. The later censuses that give the exact age and date of birth are obviously more useful, although these may not always be as accurate as one may wish.

Christian names and place names have sometimes been translated from French by the enumerators. So Jean may appear as John, and Jeanne as Jane. *Vingtaines* were often used and the map of Jersey (see page 16) shows these and can be used to identify the place of residence. There is a typed index by surname for the 1841 census at both the SJL and Jersey Archive. Lorna Pratt's transcription is not complete as the copies that she used were very faint, see: www.members.shaw.ca/jerseymaid.

The Indexes for 1851, 1861, 1871, 1891 and 1901 have been published by the CIFHS. There is some helpful information at the beginning of the indexes, including the district names and a chronology of the year. Copies were sent to the British Library, the Society of Genealogists and The National Archives and have also been purchased by the LDS and various libraries. There are transcriptions of the censuses in the CIFHS collection in the Jersey Archive.

The 1881 census is freely available through the LDS family history centres worldwide and on: www.familysearch.org and other paying genealogical websites.

Some of the censuses are also now available on the Free Census site (www.freecen.org.uk/). S&N Genealogy (www.genealogysupplies.com) have produced both the indexes and original pages on CDs.

The census for Jersey appears on all the commercial websites, but the transcriptions proved to be quite difficult as Jersey surnames caused confusion

– not only because many of the names were of French origin, but quite often the 'de' or the 'Le' are transcribed as Christian names, so, for example, 'Winter (his Christian name) de Gruchy (his surname)' appears as 'Winter Le (two Christian names) Grusky'. Some of these errors have now been corrected, but many still remain. The census transcriptions and indexes done by local volunteers are of better quality.

The 1911 census is currently available only on one site, but this will change shortly. The 1921 census will become available in due course. Unfortunately the 1931 census records were destroyed in a fire in Middlesex in 1942. In August 1940 a census for Jersey was taken, but, although the numbers are available, the names do not seem to have survived the German Occupation. However, under the Registration and Identification of Person (Jersey) Order, 1940, the entire civil population of Jersey was required to register with the authorities. The official set contains over 31,000 registration cards. Each registration card contains personal details, such as name, address, date of birth and a photograph. Any children under the age of 14 are recorded on the back of their father's card. If a person died during the Occupation, the card was removed. The registration cards have been catalogued and are available through the Jersey Archive database via a name search or under the reference 'D/S/A'. Copies can be ordered from the Jersey Archive. Identity cards were issued and these may be found in private collections.

Those who were evacuated from the island before the German Occupation in 1940 had to apply in order to return to the island and these applications are in the Jersey Archive.

Note that Jersey-born people appear on the censuses of other countries, such as Canada (which had useful records from 1851), the United States of America (from 1790), Australia and New Zealand. Some of the databases are searchable using birthplace.

Other Population Records

Earlier population counts were taken for a variety of different reasons and the information reflects this; the following is a list of those known at the present time, it is possible that others may be found, perhaps in parochial or manorial records.

Militia Censuses 1806 and 1815

During the Napoleonic wars two censuses were taken of all the men available to defend the island in the event of an invasion. General Don's militia census of 1815 predates the earliest available official British census by the best part of a generation and was undertaken in French. It has been indexed by Ngaire Ockwell of New Zealand and there are copies at the CIFHS at the Jersey Archive, as well as the SJL.

It is useful to locate the *Vingtaine* in which your ancestors may have lived; this will add a little colour to your family history, as every man's

Soldiers of the Royal Jersey Militia firing howitzers on Elizabeth Castle, c.1909

contribution to the defence of the island is given. There are likely to be a number of omissions – widows or single women as head of households, foreigners and British Army garrison troops.

The headings are as follows: name (surname, followed by Christian name); age; militia rank; parish; *Vingtaine*; Fe(mme) – women; Ga(rçons) – boys; Fi(lles) – girls. These last three columns expose the one weakness of this source – the names of wives (or other adult females) and children are not given, just the number of them in each man's family.

An entry looks like this: 'ASPLET Philippe 23 Soldat Artillerie St Peter Du Douet 1 Fe. 1 Ga.'. So, Philippe Asplet is shown as an artillery soldier, living in the Vingtaine du Douet, St Peter. In 1815 he was 23 and (presumably) married with just his wife and one son in the household. Just to demonstrate how many ways a man could make his contribution to defence (or not, as the case may be) here is a sample of the entries to be found under militia rank – excluding the obvious officer and non-commissioned ranks: *Fournit un cheval* (provides a horse) – these men were usually elderly and no longer active, often their sons are to found listed as 'Cavalier'; *Gardien* (prison guard); and *Tambour* (drummer).

An earlier survey was undertaken in 1806 but is differently arranged. The index is handwritten and organised per parish (as opposed to encompassing the whole island). Heads of households are given (and do include some females); some militia ranks are noted. However, ages are missing and women and children who were not heads of household are counted but not named.

The Inhabitants of St Lawrence 1788

In 1788 an island-wide census was taken but unfortunately only the total figures are available for the parishes – with the exception of St Lawrence. A copy of this was found among the archives of La Hague Manor, and is now in the SJL. It was reproduced in the CIFHS journals nos. 8–14 (1980–82). It gives the names and ages for the inhabitants of the parish, but does not distinguish between the households; married women appear to be listed under their maiden names.

1737 Census

This census, which was discovered in Cambridge in the 1990s, only gives the total numbers in each parish, not including St Helier or St Ouen. A photocopy of the original is in the SJL.

The Oath of Association Roll 1696

This oath was signed by Jerseymen to swear their allegiance to the Protestant King William and Queen Mary. In a book by Alex Glendinning, *Did Your Ancestors Sign the Jersey Oath of Association Roll of 1696?*, the signatures are reproduced and identified; but there is also a lot of information about the parishes and the signatories. Although other documents included signatures, this is probably the most comprehensive list for the island.

The St Lawrence Manifest 1646

Another list of men with their signatures, but only for the parish of St Lawrence, which was published by the Société Jersiaise; there is a transcript in the SJL.

Inhabitants of Trinity 1613

A list of communicants living in the parish of Trinity in 1613 was written in one of the parish register books; this was published in the *Annual Bulletin for the Société Jersiaise* for 1883; it gives the names of the heads of households and the relationship of those who lived with them, but not their names.

French Refugees

There is a microfilm copy from The National Archives, FO95/603, in the SJL of a list of French Royalist refugees resident in Jersey in 1793. An index has been made. It even includes information such as height and colour of eyes.

Chapter 5

CHURCH REGISTERS, NAMES AND CEMETERIES

The Church of England Parish Registers

The parish registers are the Church of England records of baptisms, marriages and burials for the island's twelve parishes. They are, for the most part, in French, although as they usually follow a standard pattern, they are fairly easy to understand.

All the original registers have been deposited at the Jersey Archive.

The Church of England Parish Church of St Mary, Jersey. The church dates from at least 1042. Nearby was a religious house that was burnt down during one of the many raids on the island, probably in the tenth century.

Members of the Channel Islands Family History Society have made indexes for all of them and these are available both at the archive and the SJL. All the registers have been indexed up to 1842 (the start of civil registration), and some beyond. Post-1842 baptisms for the parish of St Helier have been indexed by volunteers and are now on the Jersey Archive website www.jerseyheritage.org. The transcriptions are on several PDF files and are searchable. The indexes have been deposited both at the SJL and the CIFHS. Mistakes may have been made, so it can be important to check with the originals if there is any doubt.

The rectors can provide copies of the entries in the registers. However, as most of the registers have been deposited with the Jersey Archive, it is now possible to have a photocopy made of the entry instead. Rectors charge a fee for research, (see: www.cofe.anglican.org/lifeevents/fees/2010feestable.pdf) but as they are busy people, they may not always be able to help, particularly with lengthy or complicated enquiries. Certificates are available for a fee, if precise details are given. No bishop's transcripts of Channel Islands registers are known to be in existence, although the islands have been under the jurisdiction of the Diocese of Winchester since 1498. Previously the islands came under the Diocese of Coutances in Normandy.

The dates of commencement of the original Church of England registers are as follows:

Parish	Baptisms	Marriages	Burials
St Helier	1596	1596	1596
St Lawrence	1654	1655	1654
St Brelade	1560	1560	1560
St Peter (St Pierre dans le Désert)	1626	1626	1626
St Ouen	1634	1634	1634
St Saviour (St Saveur des Epines)	1540	1542	1542
St Martin (St Martin le Vieux)	1594	1593	1593
St John (St Jean des Chênes)	1594	1583	1581
St Mary (Ste Marie du Monastre Brulé)	1648	1648	1647
Trinity (La Sainte Trinité)	1624	1612	1612
Grouville (St Martin de Grouville)	1584	1598	1593
St Clement (St Clément de Pierreville)	1623	1623	1623

It is probable that all parishes started their registers in 1540 or thereabouts (although there is one earlier burial register for St Saviour) and that those that start at later dates have lost their earlier books. Not all the parish registers are complete; some have a few entries missing, others several years. St Lawrence, for example, is missing 1693–95 and 1700–10 has few entries. During the Commonwealth period, 1649–60, there are frequent gaps and marriages are noted as taking place *dans le temple* (in the temple, i.e. the church) as a civil ceremony rather than a religious one.

The rector tended to write down the details of a baptism, marriage or burial on a separate piece of paper and then he or a churchwarden would later write them into the register book, which may account for missing entries. Occasionally there are entries relating specifically to missing baptisms: an appeal is made to the Ecclesiastical Court who then request that a new entry is made. This was usually because a person was about to be married and required proof of their baptism. Witnesses such as the parents or godparents would be required to attest.

In 1724 the population of St Aubin in the parish of St Brelade petitioned the Bishop of Winchester to build a chapel of ease in the village, as the parish church was some distance away. Several small Church of England chapels were built in the nineteenth century, namely St Andrew, which started as a mission for sailors (the mission then moved to the Esplanade in 1872; and then to First Tower in 1926), Gouray (1833), St Matthew in Millbrook (1840), St Pierre de la Rocque in Grouville (1851) and St George in St Ouen (1876). In the twentieth century a small mission church was started with meetings in a working men's club, eventually land was purchased and St Nicholas in St Clement was built with the help of the Boot family in 1927.

When the population of St Helier became too great to be supported by one parish church, new ones were founded: St Paul (www.stpaulsjersey.org/our%20history) was the first in 1812. Later the town was divided into ecclesistical districts: St Luke in 1852, and All Saints, St Simon and St Andrew in 1872. St James was the garrison church and its registers start in 1904, and St Mark in 1917 (see: www.stmarksjersey.org/history.shtml). The registers for baptisms, marriages and burials have now been deposited in the Jersey Archive. Their marriage registers all post-date civil registration and are also in the custody of the Superintendent Registrar. St Simon's registers usefully give place of burial.

There is a register of baptisms, marriages and burials for the garrison at Elizabeth Castle, which dates from 1784 to 1817; the original is in the Jersey Archive. A photocopy and index is in the CIFHS collection and at the SJL.

The Hôpital Général (General Hospital) had a chapel from 1838 and there is a corresponding baptism register in the Jersey Archive.

Baptisms

A typical baptismal entry will give the child's Christian name, the father's name, and (from about the mid-seventeenth century) the mother's Christian name and, most usefully, her maiden name. This use of the woman's maiden name follows the French custom whereby the maiden name is always retained, and a married woman is described, for example, as 'Jeanne de la Perelle, *femme* (wife) Jean Vibert', this continues when she is a *veuve* (widow), and is used on all legal documents even to the present day.

The date of baptism is given, though this can sometimes be either the date that the child was presented at the church, or the date that the child was baptised at home; the register, usually but not always, will indicate whether it is a presentation date or a home-baptism date. If the date of presentation is not given then it is possible that the child died before this took place, so this should be checked in the burial register. The date of birth is only rarely given, although it does begin to appear in the parish of St Helier from the early nineteenth century, when English usage also begins (if the child was of English parentage). Many of the indexes prepared by family historians make frequent use of abbreviations, as often do the original records. Anyone who has no French at all could well be confused when consulting them or receiving a copy through the mail without explanation.

The following example is from Trinity, Jersey: '9.10.1625 Tho. fs Tho. Blampied (Jean Bisson fs Jean fs Barth)'. This translates as: 9 October 1625 Thomas son of Thomas Blampied. Godfather (in brackets): Jean Bisson son of Jean son of Bartholomew.

Note that the dates are in the following order: day, month and year. The first thing to remember is that this is a date of baptism and not birth. Often researchers are thrown when the date does not match up with family records (e.g. notes in Bibles, journals or letters). By the nineteenth century many rectors began to record both. Baptism could take place immediately upon birth, *à l'église* (at the church) or, if the child was sickly and not expected to survive, *à la maison* (at home) or *en particulier* (in particular – probably at the house, but possibly arranged hurriedly in the church). Sometimes you will find an entry for both. Other, more modest, families did not expect the rector to call at their homes and would wait until the child was strong enough to be taken to the church. Another reason for delayed baptism would be if the father was absent when the child was born. If he fished the Newfoundland Banks off Canada, for example, the baptism could be between three to six years late, or longer.

The registers usually include the names of godparents – this can be very useful as they are frequently relatives, and their relationship is sometimes indicated. The Calvinist Church laid down rules about godparents; normally the godfather could only be aged 14 years or over.

Until the early seventeenth century only the name of the godfather was shown, although, curiously, in the St Brelade's register it is sometimes only the godmother's name. The names of the godparent(s) appeared last and the godfather was always named. By 1625, however the mother and godmother's names were included, but they could be referred to by their husband's, fiancé's or father's names.

Baptisms of children were to be carried out no later than the next Sunday after the birth. In St Helier in the nineteenth century baptisms at the Town Church were held at 9 a.m. on Sundays and on Wednesday or Friday before or after the service.

Occupations of the father were rarely stated – except in a few cases towards the early 1840s, just before the introduction of civil registration. There are a few exceptions to this rule: doctors are mentioned, as are those who held an honorary position in the church or parish, for example

Connétable (Constable of the parish) – the most senior of the (unpaid) honorary positions, also known as the 'father/mother of the parish'; *Centenier*, the next most senior of the honorary positions, theoretically responsible for one hundred households; *Vingtenier*, theoretically responsible for twenty households; *Lecteur*, the lay reader; or *Surveillant*, the churchwarden.

Place of residence is occasionally shown; this is particularly noticeable in the parish of St Ouen, where there were many people with the same surname, so a residence or the area they lived, e.g. L'Etacq, could identify them more easily. The St Ouen registers also often give the father's parentage – a typical entry may be: 'Jean fils Jean Vibert, fils Thomas' (Jean son of Jean Vibert, son of Thomas). It is difficult to say how many baptisms have been omitted, but some parishes have quite long gaps, perhaps because there was no rector. The parishes of St Saviour, St Lawrence and St Brelade, in particular, all suffered from such absences. It is obvious that mistakes, as well as omissions (apart from the obvious gaps) were made, but it is always annoying to find the baptisms for all the other children in a family with the exception of the direct ancestor. In many cases, of course, the child may have died before baptism. In 1611 the Ecclesiastical Court suspended a man from the Lord's Supper for failing to have his child baptised before it died.

It is worth checking all the other parishes in case the child was baptised elsewhere. It should not be assumed that your ancestors were not mobile, sometimes a child was baptised in one of the other Channel Islands, England or France. Of course there are those who were born at sea and then baptised at the nearest port, perhaps in Canada or Italy, or they were baptised many years later when they returned home. The journals of the Channel Islands Family History Society include a regular column of strays, which come either from newspapers or other family history societies where a mention of Jersey has been noticed. A list of people from Jersey who married in Sark also appeared in the CIFHS journal no. 85.

In Jersey, it is worth looking at the Ecclesiastical Records to see if a remonstrance was made. This is a statement, normally made at the time of a person's marriage, when it was realised that the baptism was not in the register. For example, on 9 June 1828 it was recorded that Jean Matthews Poingdestre, younger son of the late Charles Poingdestre, Esq. and Demoiselle Elizabeth Simonet, was born in St Helier and baptised about ten or twelve days after his birth on 17 August 1801; his godparents were Jean Simonet (uncle) and Demoiselle Marie Matthews (his wife). It was noted that no entry had been made in the register. A copy of the remonstrance is usually put in the original registers, and these are sometimes found at the back of the volume.

Children who died before baptism would naturally not appear in the baptismal records, only in the burials. Stillbirths do not appear to have been recorded in Channel Island parish registers. Illegitimate children who were baptised are usually described as *né/e en paillardise* (born in wantonness), or *fils naturel/fille naturelle* (natural son or daughter). Usually the child is recorded under the mother's surname, but sometimes they are given a surname that is different from the mother's, and the assumption is made that this is the father's surname, though this may not be the case. If the parents were subsequently married, under Norman law the child would automatically be legitimised – this recognition can be noted in the parish registers. For example, in St Saviour, Jean Philippe married Jeanne Fauvel on 22 July 1801 and it is noted that *Betté Fauvel reconnu pour sa fille* (Betté Fauvel was recognised as his daughter). Betté had been baptised on 21 May 21 1801 with only the names of her mother and godparents (Josué Le Couteur and Rachel Mahaut) listed.

When an illegitimate child was born the case could be presented by the churchwardens to the Ecclesiastical Court and the mother and the father (if he has been named) would have to do penance. No check has been made to see if every illegitimate child who appears in the baptism registers also appears in the Ecclesiastical Court. In 1575 the Church Synod agreed that bastard children would be baptised if presented by a faithful godfather. Foundling children appear particularly in the nineteenth century in the St Helier records, and were given somewhat fanciful names, such as 'Jean de la Porte' ('John of the Door'), presumably because he was found outside someone's door. There was even a George Neige (George Snow) who was abandoned in February. The name 'de Jersey' was also used for these children, but it should not be confused with the prominent Guernsey family of the same name. The General Hospital baptism register and index (1838–78) is in the Jersey Archive. Many of the children baptised there were illegitimate and some are duplicated in the St Helier baptism register.

Concerns about growing poverty and the onerous duty of the parish to look after its native poor led to a discussion by the church assembly. Baptism conferred rights of residence and in 1821 the parish of St Saviour was concerned enough to refuse baptism to those children born out of the parish, although baptism could not be refused to those born in the parish.

Some churches have lists of those who were confirmed; these are now in the Jersey Archive under the individual parish.

Marriages

Registration of marriages is probably more complete than for baptisms. The entry usually includes the groom's name, the bride's name and the date. From the middle of the seventeenth century the parish of origin of the bride and groom are given but may not always be accurate. Sometimes the name of the father of the bride or groom may be shown, but this is rare. Occupations are seldom given, except in the period just before the introduction of civil registration.

Marriages could be carried out after banns, costing 5s. to 10s., had been read in the church on three successive Sundays before the wedding. Licences could also be issued: in the nineteenth century they cost from 10s. to £5 depending on the place and the hour of the ceremony. Strangers were required to enter into a bond and foreigners marrying British subjects had to obtain permission from the Governor. There is a list of declarations 1823–50 (Jersey Archive A/J/2 – an index is available) made at the time of marriage by natives of Jersey who were marrying non-natives that any children born of the marriage would not become chargeable to the parish.

Some church records for banns issued are in the Jersey Archive and there is a rare book of licences issued by the Dean 1823–30 in the Jersey Archive, (G/C/09/A3/20).

The minimum age for marriage was 14 for boys and 12 for girls, which was set by the Canon Laws of 1625. Later, probably in the nineteenth century, the age was increased to 16 for both boys and girls. Although the age was very young, it does not appear that many were actually married so young – consent of the parents was essential for juveniles, and the age of majority was 20 until 1999, when it was changed to 18.

The choice of a particular parish for the wedding can seem to be purely arbitrary. A marriage might be expected to take place in the parish of the bride or groom, but often this was not the case, and indeed the parish chosen can frequently be the furthest away from the parish of residence. It is thought that this might have been to avoid the high jinks that might otherwise accompany the wedding or the expense of a party for all the relatives and friends. So it is quite possible that a search will have to be made of all the parishes in order to find the marriage.

In Jersey this task has been made slightly easier with the gift of a computer print-out of all the marriages that took place in Jersey in the eighteenth century. It was compiled by Professor Karen Gottlieb of Pennsylvania State University – both the CIFHS and SJL have copies. This is a very valuable aid to genealogists but, as it was not compiled primarily for them, the following points should be borne in mind: there are separate indexes for male and female surnames, and, as the compiler cautions, the spelling of some of the surnames has been standardised. It should also be noted that when no parish was listed, it was assumed that both the bride and groom came from the parish in which the marriage was recorded unless there was other information (e.g. stranger or English soldier). This omission appears particularly in the earliest part of the century, and as such an assumption is obviously not correct in many cases the original registers need to be checked.

Marriages did not always have to take place in church. Members of the de Carteret family were married in Mont Orgueil Castle and sometimes the register says that a wedding took place at the home of the bride or groom. The registers occasionally record marriages that took place outside the parish. In 1842, when civil registration was established, the office of the Superintendent Registrar became available for those who did not want a religious ceremony. Non-parochial Church of England churches and non-conformist churches could apply to register marriages and this happened gradually. Under the Marriage and Civil Status Law (2001) many places could be licensed for marriages, including castles and hotels. The Channel Islands appear to have been used as a kind of Gretna Green in the eighteenth and nineteenth centuries, especially for those living in the south of England. This becomes particularly noticeable after the introduction of Lord Hardwicke's Act of 1754, which did not allow minors to marry without parental consent. Advertisements were actually placed in the south coast newspapers advising of the availability of boats to bring eloping couples across the Channel. In a similar way the Channel Islands were used when a widower wished to marry his dead wife's sister, as this was forbidden by English Canon Law. The greatest number of these marriages appears in the town registers of St Helier, although St Saviour was also to become very fashionable. This may have been because the Dean, William Le Breton (father of Lillie Langtry, mistress of King Edward VII), was also the rector of St Saviour.

During the Commonwealth period (1649–60) a number of marriages were conducted by a legal official rather than a minister, and became a civil matter. As a result many of the parishes have no marriages in their records for this period. Occasionally a copy would be made in the register – a typical entry in St Lawrence reads : *Dr Denys Guerdain se maria à la nouvelle mode à Dlle Marie Hérault le 3 novembre 1656* (Dr Denys Guerdain was married in the new manner to Dlle Marie Hérault, 3 November 1656).

The time of marriages has varied over the centuries: in the early twentieth century they often took place at 6 a.m., so that the couple could leave the island on the mail boat for their honeymoon. In the late eighteenth and early nineteenth centuries, 'marriages among all but the lower classes, are generally solemnised in the evening and at home,' says William Plees in his book *An Account of the Island of Jersey* published in 1815.

Burials

Burials should be well recorded, as disposal of a body by any other means is usually rather difficult. However, there were many instances of people drowning. If a body was recovered, then a burial could take place, but this could be several days or weeks after the drowning. Some registers record deaths of sailors who were drowned abroad – usually off Newfoundland or Portugal. Many Jersey people who died abroad would obviously not have been recorded. Three sources of information that could help would be monumental inscriptions, newspapers and the records of the Jersey Merchant Seamen's Benefit Society (see page 62).

If a death was presumed to have happened, but, for example, no body had been found, then a declaration of presumption of death could be made seven years after the presumed date of death. This was then registered in the Cour d'Héritage at the beginning of each legal term. The seigneurial courts also recorded the names of their tenants who had died without direct heirs.

Again, these were recorded in the Cour d'Héritage as well as the fief rolls of the individual fiefs. In the parish of St Brelade during the plague of 1626 many people were buried in their gardens, and this is noted in the register. There may well have also been those who had no burial service. Suicides normally were not buried in the church cemetery, so it is possible they were omitted from the registers, although this has not yet been checked.

In the register the name of the deceased is usually given, except when it was not known, such as in the case of strangers or unidentified bodies. The age of the deceased, unless exceptionally old, is rarely given, nor their occupation.

If the cause of death was unusual then this is sometimes noted; the early burial registers of St Martin in Jersey are particularly helpful in giving cause of death. For example, in 1636 an entry notes that Susanne Dolbel, widow of Nicollas Valpy, was found dead by her children, lying next to her cow – it was thought that she may have been killed by a kick from the cow and an inquest was held. When a child is buried the name of the father is usually recorded. Women are normally recorded under their maiden names; the name of their father or husband is usually given, and if they were a widow, they will be described as such.

Women who died in childbirth may have had a separate wake carried out by other women; this was stopped in 1624 by the Ecclesiastical Court. William Plees, writing in 1815 in *An Account of the Island of Jersey*, described part of the ritual surrounding a Jersey burial:

> When anyone dies, it is usual to send an early notice to relatives and particular friends; these, in return are expected to pay a visit of condolence, before the day of inhumation. The nearest in affinity to the deceased, seldom appears; some other relative receives the visitor. A general invitation for relations, friends and neighbours to attend the funeral, is then issued. A corpse is therefore followed to the grave by a numerous concourse, who, even among the lower ranks, are mostly in mourning; this indeed forms the general dress of the island: intermarriages link so many persons together, that the family connexions of everyone are extensive, and it is customary to assume the sable garb, even for an infant. The internment frequently takes place within two to three days after death, and a subsequent visit to the nearest relatives is again expected.

The earliest burial register for 1462–68 predates those given above and is for the parish of St Saviour in Jersey. For further details see *The Parish Church of Saint Saviour* by F. de L. Bois. Some parish registers, particularly that of St Martin, give other information relating to local events, such as the arrival of a new minister, or the habits of a newly buried individual, the effect of storms or threatened invasions by the French.

Apart from the registers, there are also church records that show the ownership of pews. Pews could be inherited and therefore could be sold – they gave a good indication of social status. In 1786, for example, in St Ouen both the de la Perrelle and the Ricard families had interests in seven of the pews in the parish church, and the Syvret family had five. To put this into context, there were only 101 pews listed as being in the church at that time. These records are with the Jersey Archive.

Roman Catholic and Non-Conformist Registers

After the Protestant Reformation the islands turned increasingly to the French refugee ministers as they were Calvinists and could provide a service that was more in line with the islanders' religious preferences, as well as being in French. Gradually this influence lessened, although a strong anti-Catholic feeling persisted. It was only with the influx of French refugees during the French Revolution, from about 1792, that the Catholics, including Irish Catholics, were permitted to hold services; these were held in rented rooms called oratories. There were at least four oratories in the late eighteenth and early nineteenth centuries in St Helier, including that of St Louis.

Baptisms and marriages were performed there; burial rites were usually performed in the cemetery. The first Roman Catholic chapel built in St Helier was at Hue Street in 1826. There was also the Albion Chapel, which was used by a French order. The earliest Catholic registers were kept by the Catholic Fathers in charge of the churches of St Thomas, and St Mary and St Peter in St Helier, and they have been deposited at the Jersey Archive. The St Thomas registers date from 1792 to 1901; the baptisms, marriages and burials are all mixed up together, are often only partly legible and are mainly in Latin. However, they have now been indexed and copies are at the SJL and Jersey Archive.

When the Irish arrived in Jersey they were not welcomed at the French-speaking St Thomas's Church so founded St Mary and St Peter's Church, whose registers date from 1811 and have been indexed. Other Catholic churches in the island have registers that have also been deposited at the Jersey Archive; these include St Matthew from 1872, Sacred Heart Church from 1901, Ville à l'Evêque Church from 1914 and St Anne in St Ouen from 1920. The following list shows the parish and name of church (some of these have now closed):

St Martin:	Our Lady of the Japanese Martyrs, Faldouet
Gorey:	Our Lady of the Assumption
St Peter:	St Matthew
St Ouen:	St Anne
Trinity:	St John and St Anthony
Grouville:	St Joseph
St Brelade:	St Bernadette, La Moye; Sacred Heart, St Aubin

St Lawrence: Our Lady of the Universe, Millbrook
St Clement: St Patrick

Methodists

Methodism was introduced to the island by Jerseymen who had been to Newfoundland; John Wesley visited the island in 1787. There was a French and an English circuit, and by the mid-nineteenth century there were nearly thirty chapels in the island. The Methodists' registers of baptisms date from about 1830 to the present day. Most of the records have now been deposited at the Jersey Archive and indexes are now at the Jersey Archive and the SJL.

When looking for the baptism records of the Methodist Church you will not normally find early registers in the individual chapel's name. In general, baptism registers were held for an entire circuit rather than individual chapels. The Jersey Archive holds the baptism registers for the French Wesleyan circuit from 1831, the English Wesleyan circuit from 1830 and the Bible Christian circuit from 1841. Marriages and burials were not permitted until the introduction of civil registration. Occasionally a child was baptised in both the Church of England and in a Methodist chapel.

Within the Jersey Archive Methodist collection there are hundreds of minute books of various bodies within the church, including the local preachers, trustees for individual chapels, youth clubs, choir groups and ladies' organisations. There are also registers relating to the Sunday schools and roll books that list children within the chapel as well as account books

Chapelle Wesleyenne, St Martin, Jersey, built 1851. This was one of the French-circuit Methodist chapels; the first Methodist chapel in Jersey was built in 1809.

and other papers relating to the chapel buildings. However, they are not indexed.

A rarely used record is the microfiche of the *Channel Islands District Methodist Historic Roll*; this is a part of the *Wesleyan Methodist Historic Roll*, a unique set of fifty large leather-bound volumes, which are located at Westminster Methodist Central Hall in London. The volumes contain the names of over one million people who donated a guinea to the Wesleyan Methodist Twentieth Century Fund between 1 January 1899 and September 1909 when the fund was finally closed. These records are available on microfiche at the Jersey Archive.

There is a list of some early Methodists from *Methodism in the Channel Islands* by R.D. Moore on: http://members.societe-jersiaise.org/whitsco/method0.htm.

The churches of the Independents had several registers in French and English; there are articles, which include transcriptions, on the following registers in the journals of the CIFHS: Albion Chapel no. 11, 1981; Zion Chapel no. 12, 1981; and Halkett Place no. 47, 1990 (baptisms and marriages 1809–1900). There are also registers of St John's Congregational Church (United Reformed Church), with baptisms dating from 1810 (see article in the CIFHS journal no. 39, 1988); the Independent Chapel at Maufant dating from 1850; and the Independent Chapelle des Vaux, St Brelade, starting from 1814, which are all at the Jersey Archive. Indexes for all these registers are kept at the Jersey Archive and the SJL.

Also at the Archive are baptism and burial registers for the New Church Society that was located at Victoria Street, St Helier, dating from 1844, for Halkett Place Evangelical Church, also St Helier, from 1809, La Chapelle des Vaux in St Aubin from 1914, St Saviour's Independent Church from 1851, the United Reform Church Collection (which includes registers from Zion Chapel) from 1827 and the Independent Churches of St Helier and St John from 1810. The archive records of the Presbyterian Church are also kept at the Archive, although these do not include registers.

The following list shows most of the chapels of the non-conformists; several are no longer in use:

St Helier:	Aquila Road; Wesley Grove; Vauxhall; Don Street; Wesley Street; Seaton Place
St Peter:	Bethesda; Philadélphie
St Mary:	Bethlehem
Trinity:	Ebenezer; Carmel; Augrès
St Saviour:	Eden; Georgetown; Five Oaks
St Lawrence:	First Tower; Galaad; Six Roads
Grouville:	Gorey; La Rocque; Salem
St John:	Sion; Les Frères
St Clement:	Les Tours; Samarès; Bethel
St Brelade:	St Aubin; Tabor

St Martin: St Martin Wesleyan
St Ouen: Trodez

The Bible Christians combined with the Methodists in 1907 to become the United Methodists and their chapels were as follows:

St Helier: Great Union Road; Royal Crescent
St Peter: Tesson; Beaumont
St Martin: Gorey; Les Landes

The Baptists and the Independents sometimes used each other's chapels:

St Helier: Vauxhall; Albion; Salem; Oddfellows Hall; Sion; Zoar; Halkett Place; Victoria Street; Belmont Hall; Bethel; Commercial Buildings
St Saviour: Maufant
St Clement: Les Tours
St Brelade: Les Vaux; Les Quennevais
St Peter: Les Landes
St John: St John's Congregational Church

The Church of Scotland built St Columba's Church in 1859 in St Helier, mainly for Scottish soldiers from the garrison. There was a Jewish synagogue, which has a small register held by the Superintendent Registrar; the present-day Synagogue is in St Brelade, and therefore their records are kept by the registrar of St Brelade. The first known Jerseyman who was a Quaker, Helier Dumaresq, was buried in 1670, in St Clement, but the first services were not held until 1742. There is a register dating from 1842, also in the care of the Superintendent Registrar.

Other churches or chapels include those for Swedenborgians, Jesus Christ of the Latter-Day Saints, Salvation Army, Elim Pentecostal and Jehovah's Witnesses.

Christian Names and Surnames

Most surnames started about the thirteenth century and tend to be either descriptive (e.g. Le Roux – the red haired), from a place (e.g. de Carteret) or from an occupation (e.g. Le Feuvre – the smith).

Some surnames appear to be almost unique to Jersey, such as Pipon, or of great antiquity in the island, but now rare, like Anquetil, but the majority are of Norman, Breton or British origin. Dr Frank Le Maistre's articles in the CIFHS journals nos. 2 and 3 discuss the origins of many Jersey surnames. A list of Jersey surnames appearing in many different island records was compiled by Charles Stevens, and copies are in the SJL and Jersey Archive.

In the mid-nineteenth century many Bretons and Normans came to Jersey as farm-workers; however, some of their surnames are the same as families who had been in the island for many centuries, and care should be taken to avoid confusion. An article, by Philip Stevens, on the distribution of surnames in the nineteenth century is in the CIFHS journal no. 17.

Many surnames appear to be rooted in particular parishes, such as Vibert and Le Gresley in St Ouen, Falle and Poingdestre in St Saviour. Some names that were once numerous in a parish have now completely disappeared, such as Cosnard and de la Rocque.

Occasionally, there are double surnames, such as Le Vavasseur dit Durell or Valpy dit Janvrin. The 'dit' means alias or 'otherwise known as'. It usually indicates a distinction between branches of the same family, perhaps by using the mother's maiden name, but could also be the use of a step-parent's name or may indicate illegitimacy. Some illegitimate children took their mother's maiden name, but sometimes they were known by her Christian name: there are some instances of surnames such as Marie or Jeanne. An illegitimate child might also be given their father's surname as a second Christian name.

English people have settled in Jersey since the Norman Conquest and their names occasionally became corrupted: Richardson sometimes appears as Rereson and Denton became D'Enton.

In the eighteenth century, three Jerseymen slightly changed their names so as not to be mistaken for Frenchmen (French pronunciation makes the final letter silent): the Martel, Maret and Kastel families added an extra letter at the end of their surnames and thus became Martell, Marett and Kastell.

Abroad Jersey surnames were difficult to pronounce and spell, so Le Quesne became Le Cain, Le Ruez developed into Larraway, following its pronunciation in St Helier, and Poingdestre became Poindexter. A classic example of a change of surname is that of Augustin Jean, a native of St Ouen, who, on enlisting as a soldier in the American Civil War, had his name entered as Gustin John, thus creating a new surname.

Christian names that were common in the sixteenth and seventeenth centuries included Cardin, Cosmes, Aubine or Perrine. There is a useful article on Christian names in the Société Jersiaise Bulletin for 1922, entitled 'Notes sur quelques noms de bâptemes donnés autrefois à Jersey'. Sometimes children would be given the same name as their siblings. If there is a reference to a Jean senior (*l'ainé*) and a Jean junior (*le puiné*), it could be two brothers rather than a father and son. One extreme example is that in a document of 1633, which gives the children of Richard Dolbel, who had seven daughters – three of whom were called Elizabeth and two Marie; although it is possible that they were not all alive at the same time.

When Calvinists came to the islands in the sixteenth century, they imposed strict rules on the choice of Christian names, preferring saints' names. The discipline approved at the Synod of 1576 laid down that 'concerning the names which are given to children, the Ministers will reject the names of paganism, the names of idols, and the names attributed to God in scripture: so too will they reject the names of office, like Apostle, Baptist, Angel, but rather they will admonish the fathers and godfathers to take names approved in scripture, as far as is possible.' In her book, *Old Jersey Houses*, Vol. II, Joan Stevens included an interesting analysis of Christian names 1700–1809 in two parishes: the commonest names were Jean and Marie with Philippe and Elizabeth close behind. More unusual Christian names include Winter (a surname which became a Christian name in the early 1820s and was held by a popular politican); Hedley, which was popular in St Ouen; and Garnet, the name of a popular soldier, Field Marshal Garnet Wolseley, (1833–1913). Double Christian names were rare until the end of the eighteenth century.

Cemeteries and Graveyards

Each parish church has its own graveyard, usually surrounding the church, although some later extensions are further away. For example, the churchyard around the Town Church of St Helier used to be adjacent to it, but it has been built over, and only a few of the stones were saved and placed on the grass around the church. For further information on St Helier cemeteries see: www.sthelier.je/parksandgardens/cemeteries/.

There are many memorials inside the churches, usually of wealthier parishioners; sometimes they are on the walls, though it should be assumed that the person is normally buried in the church itself. People were also buried inside the church and there are incised slabs on the floor. For example, the burial place of Major Francis Peirson, who was killed during the Battle of Jersey in 1781, is in the middle aisle of St Helier Church with a simple stone saying 'Peirson'. Until recently, it was not known if his coffin was underneath it, but recent restoration work has confirmed this. The memorial stones of the Town Church have been published in Francis Corbet's book, *The Monuments and Windows of the Parish Church of St Helier*.

Many of the church graveyards have lists and maps available from the rectors or at the Jersey Archive. The parish of St Clement has put its graveyard records on the Internet with an interactive map at: http://stclements.isgreat.org/mysql/. As well as these graveyards there are some independent cemeteries, which were opened chiefly from 1854 when it became possible to have a non-Church of England burial. Many cemeteries are no longer in use and some have been built over.

When the population increased rapidly in the nineteenth century, and there were epidemics such as cholera and typhoid, strangers' cemeteries were opened. There was a small strangers' cemetery near West Park (only a small plaque remains), and the old Jewish cemetery is adjacent to it. The Quaker cemetery was in Patriotic Street, but in 1956 land development led to the bodies being exhumed and moved to La Croix, Grouville.

When the churchyard around St Helier Church became too full (and too smelly) the Green Street Cemetery was opened in 1827. It is still in use for those who already own plots. A list of those buried there is available in the SJL and the research shelves of the CIFHS at Jersey Archive, together with information on the monumental inscriptions. All Saints was built on the site of a soldiers' and strangers' cemetery dating from 1793, and still has a few gravestones. The main St Helier cemeteries are Mont à l'Abbé (opened in 1855, with an annexe in 1881) and Surville, which opened in 1950. All of these, opened to cope with the increasing population, are situated just outside the town of St Helier. These cemeteries have different areas for different beliefs and purposes, such as the Jewish plot in the annexe to Mont à l'Abbé; some Jews are also buried at Almorah. A comprehensive record together with an index for Mont à l'Abbé is at the Jersey Archive and the SJL. Many of these indexes have been generously created by Vic Geary.

A card index for many of the graves is in the custody of the Superintendent of Cemeteries for St Helier, together with maps of the plots. Searches can be made for £10. There are individual records that include names and the funeral director, as well as the plot number. The family cards show the names of everybody in the grave, together with the name of the purchaser. For further information contact: Municipal Services Department, Parish of St Helier, Town Hall, St Helier, Jersey JE4 8PA; email: municipalservicedepot@posh.gov.je; phone: 01534 811708. The cemetery of Almorah, which opened in 1854, is also situated on the outskirts of St Helier and was originally called St Helier's General Cemetery. It was started by the Methodists, but is for any creed, with each religion having its own area. Catholics, for example, are buried in the north-east corner. There are records in the Jersey Archive and the SJL.

In 1864 a new strangers' cemetery was opened at Westmount, St Helier. It was used by the Organisation Todt (an engineering group during the Third Reich which built the underground hospital, bunkers and seawalls in Jersey using forced labour) during the Second World War; the bodies were reinterred in Normandy in 1961. This piece of land, from 1961 onwards, has been used for the crematorium; the crematorium has a book of remembrance (although it does not include all names) available for consultation. The records contain full details of the deceased as well as the place where the ashes were interred. For further information write to the Superintendent of the Crematorium: Westmount Road, St Helier, Jersey JE2 3LP; phone 01534 444880.

There are several small cemeteries that were used mainly for military burials: the Allied Military Cemetery (Second World War) in Route du Fort, St Saviour; the Russian Cemetery (1799–1801) and the British Garrison Cemetery, both on the dunes at Grouville (the latter has been built over). During the German Occupation German soldiers who died in the island were buried in St Brelade's Cemetery; in 1964 these bodies were exhumed and repatriated.

In the parish of St John there is a cemetery called Macpéla, which was used particularly for Independents and some political refugees (mainly European socialists) who had come to the island in the 1850s. There is an index, together with the records of those who were buried here, in the Jersey Archive. In St Martin there is a small Roman Catholic cemetery behind the church in the Rue au Long. Near the Trinity border is a cemetery called L'Union, which was originally opened for non-Church of England burials, but since 1952 has been run by the parish. Similarly, the La Croix Cemetery in Grouville, opened in 1853 for non-Church of England burials, is now used by any denomination. The Philadélphie Methodist chapel has a small cemetery, and so has the Trodez chapel in St Ouen, although people of other denominations are also buried in these two cemeteries.

The records of several funeral directors have now been deposited with the Jersey Archive and some have been indexed. The SJL also has some indexed records from 1823. They include details of causes of death and place of burial.

From the mid-nineteenth century church records of burials sometimes include the place of burial. For the parish of St Brelade, there is a fascinating notebook in the SJL, compiled by Joseph Farley, which dates from 1797 to 1829: it gives details of deaths and their causes, such as smallpox and accidents. He also mentions those who died elsewhere, such as Edward Orange of La Moye, St Brelade, who died in the West Indies in 1800. One of the accidents he recorded thus: '27th July 1840 Elizth. McGill poisoned by eating some Hemlock Roots that she and two other Children found in the Brook at St Helier's she died in 15 Minutes aged 7 y & ½ The other two children are under the Doctor's Hands yet still very ill.' There are many drownings and cart accidents, as well as the more unusual: 'May 24th 1840 Mr Wm. Farnham Had one of his Fingers Cut of [sic] By Doctor Grant through a Bite of Mrs Pipon of Noirmont's Dog in the Vraicing time in March.'

Monumental Inscriptions

Work has already started on recording the monumental inscriptions on gravestones in the island, and it is hoped to publish some of these in the future.

Some graves were marked by a small stone with only the initials; those in the cemetery of St John have been identified by reference to the burial registers and a copy is in the SJL.

Records for monumental inscriptions are available at the SJL for the parishes of St Peter, St Brelade (church graveyard), St Mary and part of St Saviour.

Those for the Philadélphie Chapel burying grounds in St Peter and St Ouen, and the Cimetière de L'Union, St Martin are available at the SJL.

For war memorials in the island see the records compiled by Sue Payn, which are on the CIFHS shelves in the Jersey Archive. These include not only parochial memorials, but records such as the Victoria College Book of

Remembrance. Her photographs have been deposited with the Imperial War Museum. The Channel Islands Great War Group also has lists and some photos of some of the war memorials: www.greatwarci.net/memorials/jersey/parishmems-j.htm.

Chapter 6

PROPERTY AND OFFICIAL RECORDS

Property

There are several different records on property and books that are useful for those wanting to add flesh to the history of their family. There was a high level of owner occupiers in the island, particularly in the country parishes and many families have remained in the same parish. Using information gathered from the census, it is worthwhile consulting the two volumes of *Old Jersey Houses* by Joan Stevens or looking at the histories of houses held in the Société Jersiaise Library. For architectural information on St Helier, *Buildings in the Town and Parish of St Helier* by C.E.B. Brett also includes some history of the town.

The almanacs and directories for the island give lists of local inhabitants and businesses. Unfortunately, although the modern almanacs give addresses, they no longer include names, so use can be made of telephone books instead. The Jersey Library has a good collection of these.

Many houses in Jersey have a datestone on them – sometimes known as marriage stones, they usually give initials and a date. The surname is usually shown using the main consonants: for example, Philippe Le Boutillier would be shown as PLBT. The dates can be very confusing and usually do not represent a marriage date, but rather the date when the house was built or alterations were made. An almost complete list of datestones has been collected by Joan Stevens and Alex Glendinning and can be found at: www.societe-jersiaise.org/alexgle/stonejsy.html.

Because a widow had a right for the rest of her lifetime to one third of her husband's real property (property consisting of land and buildings, as compared to personal property), there are many houses in the island that have a dower house built onto the side of the main house.

Unlike England, Jersey has had a register of property for over 400 years. Tracing the history of property is possible by using the *Registre Public* (the Public, or Land, Registry), which was set up in 1602. It is traditionally thought to have been an idea of Sir Walter Raleigh's when he was Governor of the island, but it is likely that the idea had originated before his time and he merely provided the final impetus.

Morel Farm, St Lawrence, Jersey. This farmhouse has been in the ownership of the Morel family since at least 1560, but the present house probably dates from 1716. Note the datestone over the arch: RLG 1666 – represents Raulin Langlois. It is now owned by the National Trust for Jersey. The double arch for carts and pedestrians was once common in Jersey.

Early contracts for the purchase and sale of property were conducted verbally outside the church after the service, and were called *ouie de paroisse* ('in the hearing of the parish'); eventually written documents were used, but their safekeeping was not ensured, although many can be found either in the Jersey Archive, the SJL or in private archives. Many families still have in their possession many of these contracts, including those that predate the Public Registry. In 1562 commissioners to the island suggested that a registry should be set up, and an Act was finally passed on 17 July 1602 in order to establish it. Because of the small size of Jersey the demarcation of land was considered very important, so the contracts have to record all the relevant details, which include the names of the purchaser and the vendor, and frequently their fathers' names, where the property is situated (including the parish and the fief), and usually the names of the neighbours, as well as the date and the purchase price. These contracts are therefore an extremely valuable resource for family historians as they record information that is often unavailable elsewhere. They are useful for genealogy as well, as the name of the fathers of the sellers and purchasers are usually given. Titles were also in common use, which indicated social status. *Gentilhomme* (gentleman) and *Ecuier* (esquire) indicate high status. The wife of a *Gentilhomme* or an *Ecuier* would be described as *Demoiselle* (Dlle). A lower status would be indicated by the use of *Monsieur* (Mr) or *Maîtresse* (Mse). If no title is given then that would suggest low status. Certain occupations would attract status, such as an advocate (*Ecuier*), officers in the armed forces or parish officials or honorary police (*Monsieur*). A seigneur of a fief was sometimes called by the name of his fief, for example, Monsieur de Samarès, rather than his surname.

There are some gaps in the records during the Commonwealth period (1649–60); some of the missing contracts were registered at a later date. Some contracts are in family collections available at the Jersey Archive or the SJL.

All the records of the Public Registry are in French (not Jersey Norman French); sometimes the terms used are peculiar to them, and the glossary at the back of this booklet includes some of the commonest of these words. All the original Public Registry books are in the care of the Jersey Archive and

A Jersey girl wearing a typical sun bonnet, photographed about 1929. Probably originating in the West Country of England or Brittany, the bonnet is strengthened with canes. The long piece of fabric protected the neck when milking cows.

can be studied there; there are indexes available. Until 2008 all the contracts were in French – now they are in English. The contracts from the end of the eighteenth century have been digitised and indexed (known as the PRIDE system). These can be viewed either at the Registry, which is in the States' building in the Royal Square, or at the Jersey Archive.

As these records have been recorded on microfilm by the Mormons, they are available at any Mormon library around the world, so it is not necessary to come to Jersey to see the Public Registry records. It is likely that the pre-1798 contracts will have been digitised and will be available on the Family Search website: www.familysearch.org. As any transaction that affects land has to be registered, there are a wide variety of different types of contracts. The purchase and sale of *rentes* were registered. These are small loans raised on the security of real property; formerly they were payable in kind, for example wheat or chickens, but nowadays they are payable in cash. Modern-day mortgages, known as *hypotecs*, also have to be registered. The division of property among heirs, known as a *partage*, did not have to be registered until 1840, but there are several that were recorded before this date.

According to Norman inheritance laws all the children have a share in the real property, dependent on their birth order and sex. Thus the eldest son would receive the main house and surrounding fields (known as the *préciput*), and the younger sons and the daughters would be given proportionate shares of the remainder of the land. Frequently the younger children would sell their share back to the oldest so that the farm lands would remain in the hands of one owner. However, this did not always happen, and the resulting minute subdivisions forced many of the younger sons to seek a living from the sea or away from the island. *Préciput* was abolished in 1993.

Normally, all a woman's property passed to her husband on marriage. Because the bankruptcy laws allowed creditors to sue for quite small sums, it became necessary for husbands and wives to separate their inheritances. This is known as a *séparation quant'aux biens*, after a law of 1878. These were registered in the Royal Court, but also appear in the almanacs. There has been some confusion over whether such a 'separation' is tantamount to a divorce, but it was simply to do with property ownership. The *Loi Etendant les Droits de la Femme Mariée* of 1925 changed the necessity of doing this.

Sometimes a marriage contract was registered in the Public Registry, at other times it may have been registered in the Royal Court or even be a private agreement. The Jersey Archive holds a marriage contract made in 1781 between Jean de Carteret, Seigneur of Vinchelez de Haut, and Anne de Carteret, daughter of the late Anne de Carteret who was the Dame of Vinchelez du Bas. The contract would appear to be an alliance between the two de Carteret households and includes a number of interesting clauses – for example: if Anne outlives Jean without children she keeps the furniture she brings to the marriage and also any furniture given to her; the detailed list of household goods includes red curtains, a large press of mahogany, a mirror and a bed.

The Royal Court also has records on *tutelles* (guardianships) and *procurations* (powers of attorney). The former can show the dates of death of the father and the names of his children; the guardians who were appointed were usually close relatives. A power of attorney can show where a person is living at the time and some of these have been published in the journals of the CIFHS. There are also *curatelles* (curatorships) and *enâgements* (coming of age declarations).

A large amount of property was requisitioned by the German authorities during the Occupation; the records of these are held in the Jersey Archive. Other files also include plans of land and property requisitioned.

Wills of realty (i.e. those dealing with fixed property, such as houses and land, and *rentes* and mortgages on land) did not come into existence until 1851, and are registered in the Public Registry from that date. Before that date all realty was inherited according to the laws of succession; after 1851 real property could be freely disposed of.

Wills of personalty (i.e. personal possessions, such as money, jewellery or paintings) had to be proved in the Ecclesiastical Court and there are wills that date from the fourteenth century; some may be in private collections and others have been published in the bulletins of the Société Jersiaise. Copies of these wills from 1666 have now been deposited with the Jersey Archive. Summaries of wills of personalty up to 1970 are available on www.jerseyheritage.org/research-centre/heritage-catalogues by searching on a name or by entering D/Y/A (1666–1949) or D/Y/B (1949–70) in the item reference box. Wills of personalty from 1666 to 1965 are available on microfilm from Mormon centres.

Inventories were sometimes made, separately from wills of personalty, and usually can be found in private archives; some of these have been deposited with the Société Jersiaise or the Jersey Archive.

Under the Probate (Jersey) Law 1998, article 27, all original wills and grants of probate are open to public inspection. These also include valuations of the estate of the deceased, which, however, are closed to public inspection.

Until 1948 probate was dealt with by the Ecclesiastical Court, but now the Judicial Greffe (the office of the Royal Court) handles all wills relating to personal property (i.e. cash and personal possessions), as well as dealing with such matters as adoption and divorce. As with realty, strict laws of inheritance are applicable to personal property, whether a will is left or not. In consequence there are far fewer wills of personalty than there are in England. The majority of wills were made by those who had no children, or who had property outside the island. The earliest will of personalty is dated 1670, although much earlier wills are found in family papers, and some have been published, particularly in the annual bulletins of the Société Jersiaise. It appears that as Jersey had its own Ecclesiastical Court no copies of wills were sent to the dioceses of either Winchester or Canterbury. The Greffe holds both the original wills and copies made of them. Wills that were not proved are still kept by the Ecclesiastical Court. All the wills of personalty until 1949 and, in some cases, beyond have been deposited with the Jersey Archive; the index is on their website and photocopies can be ordered. As with the Public Registry records the Mormons have microfilmed the wills of personalty, so if you have access to a Mormon library they can be consulted there.

Most wills of personalty are in French and were mainly made by single people or widows, as the laws of succession relating to the disposal of personal property were quite restrictive. An exceptional will was that made in 1742 by Marie Bartlett, née Mauger, Jersey's first woman tax collector and a wine merchant. She wrote the will herself in English and left her money for a hospital to be established for the poor, elderly and orphaned children. Unfortunately, because her English was rather poor, her cousins challenged the will and it took over twenty years before the hospital could be established.

For wills that include English property, it is possible to search the National Probate Calendar, 1861–1941, which is now available on www.ancestry.co.uk. There are over 3,000 references to Jersey on this. Copies of wills can also be ordered from the London Probate Registry at High Holborn, London. Wills of Jersey people who left property in England prior to 1858 can be found on The National Archives website in the DocumentsOnline section; this is for wills proved in the Prerogative Court of Canterbury. These also include many soldiers and sailors, but also ordinary people who may have held shares in English companies. Other wills may have been proved in English Courts, but no research has been done on this as yet.

The final Court of Appeal for Channel Islanders is the Privy Council and there are published records (mostly in English) of the Orders in Council, dating from 1536. Although many different types of cases were brought to the Council, sometimes family inheritance disputes were recorded. For example, in 1669 'Thomas Dumaresq in the behalf of himself & Coheirs on ye. one part and John Le Hardy in right of Mary Dumaresq his wife of the other part touching the succession of Richard Dumaresq the younger Brother to the said Mary and Uncle to the said Thomas' disputed the distribution of Richard Dumaresq's estate. As it had been divided unequally, contrary to Jersey succession laws, the Council ordered that it should be 'divided according to the Customes and Lawes of the said Island'.

For further information on property, there are the insurance records of the Sun Fire Office policy registers 1808–39, which are held by the Guildhall in London; the indexes are available through The National Archives website.

The West of England Insurance Company registers, 1823–1904, are indexed by place and name in the Jersey Archive website catalogue (L/A/20/A). These give details of the type of property, what it is built of, its value and, frequently, the contents. For example: 'Philip du Parcq Amy of Catillon de Bas, Grouville – On the building of a private dwelling house and wing, On offices to the West of the said dwelling house, On offices stone built and thatched adjacent to the said wing, On stables, coachouse and other offices.' Most houses had a fire or insurance mark on them, so the companies could know who to send to put out a fire. There is more information on the Le Geyt family and the fire mark on their house at: http://members.societe-jersiaise.org/history/mcfeb99.html.

Maps and plans can also be useful; for further information see Useful Local Records and Archives below. Aerial photos are a more modern source and are in the Jersey Archive and at the SJL. For a list of names of proprietors on the 1849 Godfray map of Jersey, see: www.rootsweb.ancestry.com/~jfuller/ci/1849map/intro.html.

Official Records

Since the establishment of the Jersey Archive the vast majority of official documents in Jersey are now in their care and access to them is in person or, for some documents, through their website: www.jerseyheritage.org/research-centre/heritage-catalogues. The Jersey Archive is the depository for official records for the island; these include the records of the Lieutenant Governor, the Bailiff, the Royal Court and the States of Jersey, as well as those of the parishes and churches and a lot of private material.

The records of the Royal Court deal with all civil and criminal matters that came before the various courts. The civil records are divided into different sections according to the type of action; they are for the most part in French, and are not indexed until the end of the eighteenth century. The earliest court records in Jersey were destroyed when the Bailiff's house was burnt down around 1502.

La Cour d'Héritage deals with real property, i.e. land, houses and matters of inheritance. The records date from 1506 and continue through to the present day; they include lists of those who died without direct heirs.

La Cour de Câtel is no longer in use; its records are from 1504 to 1861, and it dealt with matters appertaining to personal property. However, it also dealt with witchcraft accusations; these started in 1562, and the last case appears to be in 1765. Both men and women were accused. Marie Esnouf was accused in 1648: she was shaved by a surgeon, and when no mark was found on her body she was ordered to open her mouth. In there on her palate the Devil's mark was at last located. Then she was pricked with a lancet but stated that she felt no pain. These two signs and the written allegations of the witnesses were enough to convict her and she was sentenced to be hanged then strangled, then finally burnt in the marketplace. Curiously the most famous Jersey person connected with witchcraft was Philip English: baptised in Trinity in 1651 as Philippe Langlois, he went to Salem in Massachusetts and became a wealthy merchant. In 1692, however, he became caught up in the Salem Witch Trials and fled to New York.

La Cour du Samedi usually used to sit, as its name suggests, on a Saturday, but now sits on a Friday. It deals with all general civil cases not covered by the other courts, and its records began in 1535 and proceed to the present day. La Cour du Billet became a separate division of La Cour de Samedi from

1648, but it discontinued in the 1950s. Cases of arrears and small debts were heard by this court.

Crimes like bigamy would be tried in the Cour du Samedi; for example, Honorine Valerie Jacqueline married Jean Nicolas Risbecq from Beneville, Côtes du Nord, Brittany, on 30 January 1866 at Trinity Church. Just over a year later, with slightly different Christian names, Eleonore Honorine Jacquelin married Jean François Nicolas Duchemin from St Lô, Normandy on 7 May 1867 at St Saviour's Church. On 4 September 1867, only a few months after her second marriage, she appeared in the Royal Court charged with bigamy. Honorine was sentenced to six months in prison with forced labour.

Records of *décrets* (bankruptcy) date from 1616 to 1900 and are full of interesting details, as they have to include all property owned and all goods. They are indexed by name and are in the Jersey Archive. One bankruptcy is that of Pierre Marett in 1755, which gives a full inventory of his haberdashery business, including lists of fabrics.

The *Vicomte* is the executive officer of the Royal Court and, amongst many other duties, undertakes inquests. Inquest records are in the early court records, but more modern ones are not readily available, unless there is a personal connection to the deceased. The easiest route for looking at inquests is to read the reports in the local newspapers, which usually cover them fully. Death certificates give the *Vicomte's* verdict in the 'cause of death' column in the case of an inquest.

States of Jersey Records

The States of Jersey evolved from the Royal Court during the sixteenth century. The *Actes* of the States have been published by the Société Jersiaise covering 1524–1799. Later *Actes* are published in volumes available in the SJL or Jersey Library. All the records of the States have been deposited in the Jersey Archive. Until 2005 the States formed committees to deal with matters in hand; these include defence and education. Most of the committee records are in French and have not been indexed. For example, the Comité de l'Hôpital Général (General Hospital Committee) has records dating from its establishment in 1741; it was used as a poor house and the books include names of inmates. (Their diet is given, indicating at one point a change from beer to cider, as this was the preferred local drink.) Admission registers are also available.

Parochial Records

The island of Jersey is divided into twelve parishes and further subdivided into *vingtaines*, or *cueillettes* in St Ouen. It is the parish and *vingtaine*, rather than an address, that are given on birth certificates. (See map of Jersey).

The Jersey Archive has all the parish records, which include minutes of the parish assembly, minutes of the roads committee, lists of property transfers within the parish, maps and plans, and rates lists and schedules.

The administration and policing of the parish is carried out by the Constable, *Centeniers*, *Vingteniers*, Constable's officers and the administrative staff. The Constable was responsible (until very recently when welfare payments were centralised) for the welfare payments to the poor of the parish, there being no central poor-relief system – although this was originally a duty of the churchwardens, who may still distribute some church funds.

Revenue for the parish is raised by means of the rates, which are based on the rentable value of the property, and are expressed in *quarters* (a measurement of wheat). Each parish fixes the rate per *quarter* on an annual basis. Rating lists are produced annually and some of these go back to the eighteenth century. The earliest one found so far is for St Helier and is dated 1691. The parish of St Saviour has lists for 1718, 1751 and 1770, and there is an island-wide rating list for 1737 – a copy of which is in the collection of the Channel Islands Family History Society at the Jersey Archive. The rate lists are available in the parish halls and in the SJL and the Jersey Library. Electoral lists are also available.

The police system in the island relies on honorary officers, the *Centeniers* and *Vingteniers*, and until 1853 was the only police force. In that year a paid police force was set up in the town of St Helier. Later a States Police force was formed: they are used in cases of serious crime in any part of the island. All cases for prosecution, however, have to be presented by a member of the honorary police.

Ecclesiastical Court Records

The Ecclesiastical Court is still in existence although its powers are not as extensive as they once were. The records date from 1553 and show just how much influence the church in Jersey had over the lives of the ordinary people. It dealt with the wrongdoings of the members of the church and the laity, dealing with matters of moral misdemeanours, such as illegitimacy and non-attendance at church. In 1629, for example, Marie, daughter of Jean Grandin, was presented to the court by the churchwardens of Trinity for having spent a night locked in with an English soldier; she had to do penance in the church.

Some baptisms and marriages that had been omitted from the registers are recorded in the court records when the court was requested to do so by the people affected. Often couples who were married were brought to the court for having slept (or lived) together before their marriage; this is described as *ayant anticipé le bénédiction de mariage* (having anticipated the blessing of marriage). Cases of breach of promise of marriage also appear quite frequently. In 1635 Guillemette Blancpied was freed of her promise to marry Thomas Robert, notwithstanding that she had been given clothes by him; these had to be returned to him.

The books contain details of the witch trials that took place in the sixteenth and seventeenth centuries. More mundane matters, such as visits to parish churches and inspections of the fabric of the building, as well as swearing-in of public officials and public notaries, are all recorded in the Ecclesiastical Court records. Until 1949 the Ecclesiastical Court had to prove all wills of personalty, and although this duty has now been handed over to the Judicial Greffe, the court still retains copies of those wills that were never proved, usually because they were later altered.

There was no Divorce Act in Jersey until 1949, but before this date requests for separation could be made to the court. Separations as *a mensa et thoro* (from bed and board) could be granted only in cases of adultery, cruelty or danger of life, though this was extremely rare. One example in 1611 concerned a sailor, Thomas de la Perelle from St Ouen, who requested and was granted a divorce from his wife Sara de Laic, on the grounds that he had been captured by pirates and held for two and a half years. On his return to Jersey he discovered that his wife had not only committed adultery but had also had a child by her lover, and in fear of punishment she had fled the island.

These records are all in French, and for the most part are not indexed; they have been deposited with the Jersey Archive. There is a microfiche copy available for the records of 1623–40, with a transcript by Helen Evans, which is the SJL.

Apart from the parish registers and the Ecclesiastical Court records, each church has its own records, which include, for example, the minutes of the meetings of the *surveillants* (the church wardens). For a detailed look at these, see *The Parish Church of St Saviour, Jersey* by F. de L. Bois. The early St Lawrence records, for example, give considerable detail of the reasons why people were given money. There are instances of great need, illness and the need for money to pay for furniture and clothes. It even details money paid for people to foster children for a month in order to relieve their parents. In 1741 one of Elie Romeril's children was looked after for a month by the wife of Philippe Le Brun and she was paid four *livres* for doing this. Similarly in the same month another of Elie Romeril's children was looked after by Elie de Gruchy's wife.

German Occupation

There are many useful books on the history of the German Occupation of Jersey. Of particular interest to family historians are: *No Cause for Panic* on the evacuees and *Islanders Deported* with lists of names. In the Jersey Archive there are the registration cards of islanders deported to German internment camps (D/S/A/13). There is also a list of them compiled by Joe Mière on: www.thisisjersey.co.uk/hmd/html/570.

Organisation Todt brought forced labour to the island from many different countries. There were Russians, Moroccans, Belgians and others;

quite a number died in the island. Some of them, including a number of Spaniards, stayed in the island after the Occupation.

Earlier Records

Several medieval records, which are in The National Archives or which were in the records of Normandy (unfortunately the originals were destroyed when St Lô was bombed during the Allied invasion of 1944), were published by the Société Jersiaise. Jersey was divided into fiefs in the medieval period and the records include the published *Extentes* of 1274, 1331, 1528, 1697, 1668 and 1749, which show the owners of land and houses on the Crown fief and give details of how much was due to the Crown. The Crown lands covered about half the island. For the private fiefs there are *appairements*, some of which are in the SJL. The last vestiges of the feudal system were only abolished in 1966, although the *seigneurs* still have to swear their fealty to the Crown at the annual Assize d'Héritage.

The rolls of the criminal assizes that were held in the islands in 1299 and 1309 have also been published by the Société Jersiaise. These are fascinating documents, describing crimes such as trying to pass off dogs as sheep in the market, as well as attacks and theft.

Chapter 7

EDUCATION, EMPLOYMENT AND CRIME

Education

The earliest teachers in the island were monks who would take on pupils, perhaps in the hope that they might become monks in their turn. Schools were parish based from the sixteenth century, although there were also two grammar schools, St Mannelier in St Saviour and St Anastase in the parish of St Peter, which were founded in 1477 and 1496 respectively. The rectors of the parish churches may have also done some teaching.

Scholarships were offered for Jersey boys, especially to Exeter College at Oxford. Jerseymen, and later women, can be found in the records of universities, such as Oxford and Cambridge, which are available, for example, on the Ancestry website (ancestry.co.uk).

Until the mid-eighteenth century the parish schools were the only ones, although several attempts were made to establish a college. The teachers were licensed by the Ecclesiastical Court, with their names appearing in their

The parochial school of St Mary, Jersey, built in 1900 for children up to the age of 14. Note the signs above the doors: Garçons *(Boys) and* Filles *(Girls).*

records. For example, Mr Jean Dorey was presented by the Rector of Trinity, Monsieur Pierre Joubaire, as the master for the school of the parish of Trinity, on 31 May 1756.

Children from middle classes would be sent to be educated in France, particularly Caen. William Chepmell, born in Jersey in 1755, was sent to Caen; however, on his way to college he was kidnapped by nuns who loved him so dearly that they refused to let him return home – it took quite an effort from his uncle to have him released. A school in Romsey, Hampshire, was popular and boys were often sent just for a couple of years in order to learn English. In the early nineteenth century, the future wife of the rector of St John was sent to a school in Mile End, London, where she learnt needlework and cookery. Curiously, she had to take a silver spoon with her; one was engraved with her initials 'NFV' (Nancy Fauvel) and remains a prized possession in the family.

Later schoolmasters tried to set up schools – particularly to teach navigation – and the parochial monopoly was gradually broken. Many private schools set up all over the island, offering different subjects. Small dame schools were popular, as well as specialist teaching, such as fencing offered by impoverished French Royalist refugees from the 1790s. Non-fee-paying ones, which relied on charitable donations, started in the 1780s and they gradually increased in number. It was not until 1870 that the States of Jersey asked the British Government for assistance with establishing parish primary schools for all children. The extant school log books date from this time and are in the Jersey Archive. They include information on the subjects taught, classes missed because of bad weather, as well as the names of children and teachers.

Secondary schools were also established, with Victoria College for boys founded in 1846 with the intention of providing an education for future colonial or commercial careers. Many of the boys were English and a boarding house was also provided. Other schools followed in a similar way and in the census one sees, for example, boys from army families who were born in India boarding in schools in Jersey. The Methodists started a college for girls, the Jersey Ladies' College, in 1875. The Colleges have published lists of pupils, which are available from the SJL as well as College magazines.

The Catholic community, both French and Irish, had grown steadily since the 1790s and by 1860 there were 5,000 who attended service at the French Catholic cathedral of St Thomas in St Helier, as well as many scattered through the countryside. An invitation was extended to a community of nuns, the Dames de St André, who established a school in the island; shortly afterwards, the De La Salle Brothers were invited to open a school. In the early 1880s French education was secularised and several orders came to the island and set up schools – chief amongst these were the Jesuits who bought the Imperial Hotel and renamed it Maison St Louis; it became a seminary and later they established a naval college (Notre Dame de Bon-Secours) for French students at what is now Highlands College.

The vast majority of the records of these religious orders were actually sent back to the main bodies back in France. Similarly a lot of the records of Catholic schools that used to exist in the island are not held at the Jersey Archive, although De La Salle school has deposited their collection, which dates from 1917. Small schools were set up in the countryside, such as that of St Matthew in St Lawrence. Three Roman Catholic schools, De La Salle, Beaulieu and FCJ (*Les Fidèles Compagnons de Jésus*, Faithful Companions of Jesus), remain to this day. The *Jersey Catholic Record* was a magazine published from 1959 and gives much information about the life of Catholics in the island, as well as the history of Catholicism in Jersey.

Doris Carter in her book, *A Jersey Childhood*, has a most interesting chapter on education at *L'École Paroissiale* (parish school) at the beginning of the twentieth century. She explained that although most of the children in Jersey, particularly in the country parishes, spoke Jèrriais, when they went to school 'they had to adopt a foreign language. English was seldom spoken in the home – but infant teachers were so dedicated, gifted and hard working that the transition from Norman-French was barely noticeable, and few children moved on to Standard I without being able to read both English and French.'

Sunday schools were a well-loved feature of island life and many Sunday-school outings in the traditional Jersey van were the highlight of children's lives. Information about the Sunday schools appears occasionally in parish magazines, particularly those for the Church of England or the Methodists. There are collections in the SJL and the Jersey Archive.

During the German Occupation several schools were evacuated to England – Victoria College, for example, was re-established in Bedford School – but the majority of the schoolchildren stayed. Some attempt was made to teach them German, but most children resolutely refused to learn the language.

Orphans or abandoned children were cared for in the Hôpital Général. Their names are in the records of the hospital, which are in the Jersey Archive. There was a hospital school for them; when old enough, they were apprenticed. For example, in 1819 John Murphy, aged 12, was placed with Philippe Picot until the age of 20 on condition that he would be provided with food, lodging and religious education in return for working for Philippe.

A female orphans' home was opened in Grouville in 1858, and the Industrial School was opened in 1867 to train boys for agriculture or seafaring. Dr Barnado visited Jersey in 1879 to set up a home: this was Teighmore at Gorey, St Martin. In 1881 there were 121 children in the home. There is a list of boys who were there in 1917 in the SJL. The home included a cottage hospital, a school and a farm training centre. The Roman Catholics opened up a crèche for orphans and other children, the Sacré Coeur, in 1901 at Summerland in St Helier and had ninety-one children in their care in 1904. They taught girls sewing, an enterprise that eventually developed into the Summerland factory.

The Jersey Archive has a large collection of education archives, including the appointments of teachers, apprenticeship grants, admission books and accounts.

Individual school log books are most useful and often give the names of the children who were admitted. They have not been indexed, so it can take a while to look through them.

Employment

Although there were, of course, many farmers and fishermen in the island, there was also a large variety of occupations. Many people would have had a number of occupations: a carpenter might do some farming and fishing, as well as making furniture or coffins. As the climate was mild and the soil fertile, islanders could feed themselves well, and fish were particularly useful as a supplement in the winter. Eels and lobsters were exported during the medieval period and corn was sold to the Spaniards in the sixteenth century. *Vraic* (seaweed) was used as fertiliser and even in the nineteenth-century censuses several people are described as 'vraic collectors'. Fields were enclosed probably from the thirteenth century onwards, but this increased in the sixteenth century and cider apple trees were widely planted. These required high stone walls (*banques*) and hedges to shelter the trees, which give the island its distinctive look that prevails to this day. Cider was exported in large quantities. The Royal Jersey Agricultural and Horticultural Society was founded in 1833 and its records are with the Jersey Archive.

Knitting was introduced about the end of the fifteenth century to provide work for the poor, but soon Jersey knitted goods, including stockings and waistcoats, became well known and were exported to France and Spain as well as England. There were parochial schools to teach the skills required. The wool had to be combed and dyed, so occupations such as wool comber or dyer continued through the centuries, and occasionally can be found in the census.

Because of the privileges granted to the islands by successive monarchs (in the same way that towns in England were also granted them), the islands enjoyed certain tax privileges and from the thirteenth century onwards took advantage of this. If there was a tax on a raw material, such as wood or leather, being imported into England, then Jersey would import that material, process it (by making boots or building ships, for example), and then export the finished article, which was free of tax. Trade was the mainspring of the island's economy, whether it was exporting or importing or carrying goods around the world.

Two useful books on the maritime history are: *A People of the Sea: The Maritime History of the Channel Islands* and *From Sail to Steam*, which give a lot of information covering the whole range of maritime activities of islanders.

The cod-fishing industry probably started off the Banks of Newfoundland

This postcard shows men packing the early potatoes for export to England. The Jersey Royal was first grown from 1872 and today more than 30,000 tonnes are exported every year.

by at least the end of the sixteenth century. Soon Jersey ships established 'rooms' there and sold the fish to Spain and Portugal. Charles Robin of St Aubin, Jersey, established one of the largest cod-fishing companies in Gaspé, Canada, in 1766. He employed many Jerseymen and his firm continued to do this until at least the 1930s, although cod fishing had suffered a setback in the 1870s when the Banks were opened to all nationalities, including Americans. The Canadian censuses for 1861 show many people born in Jersey.

The privateering and smuggling activities of Jersey irritated both Cromwell and Napoleon, who were disparaging about the island. Cromwell called the island 'that nest of vypers', which is also the title of a useful book by local maritime historian Alec Podger, which includes a list of smugglers and their confiscated ships. During the English Civil War Jersey remained loyal to the Royalist cause and became a centre for privateering against the Parliamentarians. Jean Chevalier, who lived in St Helier, wrote a diary, 1643–51, which gives a great deal of information on this period; it has been transcribed and an English translation is in the SJL.

For information on shipping and privateering see: http://doug-jersey.freeservers.com/Patrimoine%20des%20Ctes.htm. This site includes a chronology of privateering, which was licensed piracy. When England was at war, Jersey ships could attack enemy ships and take their cargoes. Many Jerseymen, however, were taken prisoner – some were captured by the pirates of Sallee, Morocco and were held to ransom. One example was Pierre d'Auvergne, who was captured in 1625 en route to the cod banks off

Newfoundland. His brother-in-law managed to raise the money and take it to Morocco, only to find that Pierre had died.

During the French Revolutionary and Napoleonic wars Jerseymen were held prisoners in France. A list of these has been published in the CIFHS journal no. 43. Jersey prisoners were usually better treated as they acted as translators.

For lists of shipbuilders, harbourmasters, merchants, privateers, shipowners and much more, see: *Jersey Sailing Ships* by John Jean.

James Brannan has a website on his family history that also shows how to trace Jersey mariners and ships: http://pagesperso-orange.fr/jbrannan/ships.htm. For the Jersey Merchant Seamen's Benefit Society, see: http://members.societe-jersiaise.org/alexgle/JMSBS.html. This society, which started in 1836, has records held in the SJL, showing details of the monies received and paid out in pensions to sailors, and their names; sometimes ages and places of origin are also given. It is particularly useful as it gives details of the deaths of seamen and subsequent payments to their widows. A database has been created and enquiries should be made to the SJL. It should be noted that the entries refer to Jersey-owned ships but the sailors came from all over the world.

For general websites on shipping, which include Jersey, see: Maritime History Archives, Memorial University of Newfoundland (www.mun.ca/

St Helier Harbour with the magnificent Gladiateur *built in 1866 in Jersey by Daniel Le Vesconte. In the background can be seen Fort Regent built from 1806 for the English garrison on the Mont de la Ville.*

mha/) and National Maritime Museum, Greenwich, England (www.nmm.ac.uk/).

During the nineteenth century Jersey ships could be found in ports all over the world: Valparaiso, Buenos Aires, Rio de Janeiro, Havana, Adelaide, Sydney, Melbourne, Hong Kong, Shanghai, Karachi, Bombay, Cochin, San Francisco, New Orleans – as well as Newfoundland, the Gaspé, New England, Cadiz, Opporto, Malta, Marseilles, Naples, Constantinople and a vast selection of French and British ports.

There are ships' logs in the Jersey Archive and paintings of many Jersey sailing ships are held by Jersey Heritage (see Directory); some are on display in the Maritime Museum. One of the most interesting is that of the voyage of the *Prospero*, captained by George Malzard of St Peter, which in 1864 voyaged for over 2,000 miles up the Amazon to Iquitos – the first British ship to do so. There is a street in Iquitos called 'Prospero' after the ship.

Shipbuilding reached its zenith in 1864 when Jersey became third largest of the shipbuilding centres of the British Empire (thirty-eight ships built that year). Many men were employed in the shipyards and several ropewalks were built; they are remembered as place names, for example La Corderie in St Helier.

The Chamber of Commerce, founded in 1770, has extensive records, which are at the Jersey Archive, giving a great deal of information on the shipping industry of Jersey and giving names of shipowners. The Chamber was only the second in the English-speaking world.

The shipping industry meant that there were many merchants, artificers, carpenters and coopers in the island. There were also the usual occupations such as butchers, grocers and shoe- and boot-makers. For tax reasons bootmaking was not just for the local market – using leather imported from France, many of the boots were then exported to the American colonies and Canada. There were a variety of female occupations, some of which are mentioned in the censuses, mainly connected to clothing. Having both a port and a garrison, there were, of course, prostitutes in St Helier: they can sometimes be identified in the criminal records or in the newspaper accounts.

Smuggling was an important part of the island's economy, but there are few records that give names of those who took part. Smugglers would carry goods from France to the island and then on to England. A customs officer was appointed in the seventeenth century, but it is likely that he would have dealt with goods coming into the island and raising the relevant dues, rather than regulating the illegal transport of goods from Jersey to Devon, Cornwall and Dorset in particular. Dorset has an educational smuggling website: www.dorsetsea.swgfl.org.uk/index2.html. This website mentions the ports of Bridport, Poole and Weymouth, which all had strong connections with the Channel Islands. The customs and excise books are held by the Jersey Archive and include, for example, a list of merchants' names and ships for those trading with Portugal (D/H/B3).

The head of the island was the Bailiff, although this became a hereditary position in the eighteenth century and he would often be absent, appointing lieutenants in his place, as did the Governors, both of whom were appointed by the Crown. Other court officials include the Attorney General, the *Vicomte* and the Greffier. There are lists of all these, as well as the names of the Constables and rectors of the parishes, published in the bulletins of the Société Jersiaise.

Other professionals include doctors (the first Jerseyman to be a doctor, Soloman Journeaux, was funded by the Constables), dentists (one of the earliest was a French lady, Madame Papu) and Advocates and Ecrivains (lawyers). They had to be sworn in by the Royal Court and can be found in the Cour de Samedi records, although there are manuscript lists of these in the SJL. There are lists of many of these on: http://members.societe-jersiaise.org/lepivert/index.htm and details of the clergy can be found on: www.theclergydatabase.org.uk/index.html.

Originally established as the St Helier Fire Brigade, the Jersey Fire Brigade was set up in 1901 to cover the whole island and all the original logs are now with the Jersey Archive, including photographs of the firemen. The honorary police force dates from the fourteenth century and its records can be found in the Jersey Archive. There are also lists of names in the almanacs. For the St Helier Paid Police, now States of Jersey Police, see: www.jersey.police.uk/about/history.html. Some of their records, along with some research notes and photographs, have been deposited in the Jersey Archive, but there are also references to the police in the States records.

Specialist occupations, such as silversmiths, are covered in two books: *Makers and Dealers of Channel Islands Silver and their Marks* by F. Cohen, and *Old Channel Islands Silver, its Makers and Marks* by Richard Mayne. There is also a website: www.silvercollection.it/CHANNELISLANDSSILVERUNI.html. Pewterers are covered in *Pewter of the Channel Islands* by Stanley C. Woolmer and Charles H. Arkwright and *An Introduction to Channel Islands Pewter* by G.J.C. Bois.

Hospitality has an ancient history in the island; monks would have provided accommodation for travellers, and public houses had to have spare beds for people staying in the island. When Charles II came to the island in 1649, there was a scarcity of accommodation and members of his party had to be put up in private houses. The garrison also had to be housed privately until accommodation was built. Tourists started to visit the island, particularly from France and England, once the Napoleonic war ended in 1815. Hotels were built and boarding houses opened; steamers came to the island and guide books were written. In the twentieth century the island had a boom with English tourists, many of whom were employees of British Rail, as Jersey was the furthest they could go on their free travel concession. Because of a tax advantage many newlyweds came from England for their honeymoon. Hotel employees came from France, Italy, Portugal and Poland; and tourists came from all over Europe. In the late 1990s there were over 1,000 restaurants and cafés in the island.

The Grand Hotel, St Helier, Jersey. Facing Elizabeth Castle this hotel was originally the Alexandra and Eugenie Baths, built in the mid-nineteenth century. In 1891 the new Grand Hotel was built and still stands on the site to this day.

The Jersey Archive has a large collection of business archives, including shops such as A. De Gruchy & Co., which was established in 1824 and is still trading. There have been many societies formed in Jersey, particularly since the beginning of the nineteenth century and most of them have good records, and a number of these records have been deposited at the Jersey Archive. The Freemasons have several lodges as well as the Jersey Masonic Museum and Library, which was established in 1859 and is the oldest such institution in Great Britain – see: www.jerseymason.org.uk/craft_library.html and for research into individual members see: www.freemasonry.london.museum/family-history.php.

The care of the poor was, until 2008, the responsibility of the parish, either through the church or the municipality. There was no equivalent to the Poor Law in England and therefore no place of settlement rules or union workhouses. However, there was an attachment to the parish of birth. In the parish the *charité* records of the church list payments made – these are in the Jersey Archive. Rates were raised from the end of the sixteenth century and payments made by the parish to the poor; sometimes in kind. Such records are in the parochial records in the Archive. Problems arose when strangers – for example, widows and children of soldiers in the garrison – had to be looked after: all the parishes had to pay for them so that they could be cared for in the Hôpital Général. Their records are in the Jersey Archive and there is a list of patients for 1773–99 there, as well as a book of baptisms. There are some instances of strangers being returned to their place of settlement in England; these records appear in individual county records and can be found on The National Archives website. The Roman Catholics in the nineteenth and twentieth centuries established nursing homes and orphanages.

Crime

The Royal Court records (in the Jersey Archive) give details of criminals and their crimes; these can be found in the Cour de Samedi and the Poursuites Criminelles, 1797–1981. Originally many criminals were banished from the island; a prison was established in Mont Orgueil Castle and prisoners would be taken from there to the Royal Court in St Helier, escorted by *halberdiers*. Being a *halberdier* was a duty attached to a property, normally those in St Martin, Grouville and St Saviour. There are lists of *halberdiers* in the SJL and many still have their halberd (a type of axe on a long pole), all of which are of a distinctive pattern. Some private houses also had lock-ups, as did St Brelade's *hôpital*.

A prison was built at Charing Cross, St Helier, in 1686, which included a debtors' prison; a new prison was built in what was to be called Newgate Street, next to the Hôpital Général, in 1814 and the present prison is at La Moye, St Brelade. There are records of the Newgate prison dating from 1814 in the Jersey Archive, which give details of the criminals and their crimes; these included theft, assault and threatening a man's life. Prisoners could be sent to their country of origin, as well as being transported to Australia or to prison hulks. There is an index, but it does not include all the information. Debtors are also listed, including Mr Turpen who in 1815 escaped by climbing over the rails. Elizabeth Fry, the Quaker reformer, on a visit in 1836 said of the prison: 'finding the Prison in a shocking state showing the extremity of sin'. A 'house of correction' was founded in 1838 adjacent to the prison. The Channel Islands Female Penitentiary, in St Helier, was a prison, but also a refuge for women who had committed minor crimes. In 1863 it had twenty-five inmates who were employed in washing and needlework. There are photographs of prison warders in 1934 and of prostitutes in the Jersey Archive collection.

In The National Archives there are some records, PCOM 3/20, which refer to prisoners convicted in Jersey: nos. 1951–2050. For example, Licence number 2045: John McAuliffe convicted of Making and passing base coin at the Royal Court of Jersey at St Helier Jersey, Channel Islands, 01 September 1851; then aged 21 years and by trade None. Sentence: 7 years' transportation.

Chapter 8

MILITARY AND MIGRATION

The Militia, the Garrison, Soldiers and Sailors

The Royal Militia of the Island of Jersey dates from about the thirteenth century. Feudalism involved providing men and arms for military service and Jerseymen performed this service from the earliest times. In 1337 the Jersey militia were re-formed. Service was unpaid and compulsory for all able-bodied men from the age of 16 to 45. In 1730 there were five regiments made up of six battalions as follows: 1st – St Ouen, St Mary, St John, 2nd – Trinity, St Martin, 3rd – St Saviour, Grouville, St Clement, 4th – 1st/4th St Helier, 2nd/4th St Lawrence, 5th – St Peter, St Brelade. There were many changes over the centuries, but it survived until 1929, when it became a small volunteer force. There is a website that includes a roll of honour and information on insignia on: www.jerseymilitia.co.uk. Today there is a Royal Engineers unit based at La Collette, which is called the Jersey Field Squadron RE (RMIJ).

There was resistance to service in the militia from the Methodists, who did not wish to practise on Sundays; eventually they were exempted, though they had to do their service on another day. The militia would have summer camps on the dunes at St Brelade. There are many photographs of the militia in the collection of the Société Jersiaise as well as some in the Jersey Archive. There are also some attestation forms in private archives deposited with the Jersey Archive. The almanacs from 1797 include names of the officers in the militia. There is a display of militia silver at Elizabeth Castle. Note that the militia lists were compiled on the orders of the Lieutenant Governor General Don for 1806 and 1815.

Jerseymen have served in the British Army and Navy over the centuries and their service records can be found in The National Archives. It was said that the Channel Islands were the ideal training for sailors – this was because of the difficult local waters with strong currents, many rocks and with as much as a forty-foot rise and fall between high and low tide. Many men from the island distinguished themselves, such as Rear-Admiral Philip Carteret who circumnavigated the world in 1766.

During the nineteenth century, both Jerseymen and English men who settled in the island joined the army and served all over the world, particularly in Afghanistan. Lieutenant Colonel Ferdinand Le Quesne, who was a surgeon, won a Victoria Cross in 1889 in Burma. Five Old Victorians (former pupils of Victoria College) also won the Victoria Cross, including the two Sartorius brothers.

During the First World War many men volunteered for the British Army and joined directly. Service records for Jerseymen and women who served with the British forces are with The National Archives or with the relevant service.

A 'pals' company' of 250 volunteers was formed in December 1914 and they left on 2 March 1915 for training in Ireland. They took part in the Battle of Cambrai in 1916 and were attached to the Royal Irish Rifles, then later to the Hampshire Regiment. For further information and lists of those who took part, see *'Ours': The Jersey Pals in the First World War* by Ian Ronayne. The Channel Islands Great War Study Group has an interesting website (www.greatwarci.net) with a lot of information and they are always grateful for more. Altogether about 1,200 Jerseymen were killed during the First World War. There are memorials to many of them published in the *Jersey Evening Post*. There is also the roll of honour and service, which was published in 1919.

Two thousand Frenchmen living in Jersey enlisted in the French Army and information on them may be found in French departmental archives as well as the military archives at Vincennes: www.servicehistorique.sga.defense .gouv.fr/, although there are no indexes so information on the soldier (or sailor) has to be quite specific.

There were German prisoner of war camps at Les Blanches Banques, St

Church parade of the British garrison to the Garrison Church of St James in St Helier, Jersey, c.1910

Brelade, and several men died in the island; their deaths should be registered in that parish.

There have been garrisons in the island since at least 1204. The Medieval Soldiers database (www.icmacentre.ac.uk/soldier/database/) gives lists of those who served in the islands. Other names of those who were stationed at Mont Orgueil Castle are in the annual bulletin of the Société Jersiaise. Many men married local girls and stayed in the island, these include, for example, Whitley and Denton. Several of the battalions garrisoned were composed of invalid soldiers, as intense active service was not envisaged. Lists of the regiments are available in the SJL. Note also the garrison registers mentioned in the chapter on parish registers.

One of the earliest portraits of a black man in a heroic role is that of the Jamaican, Pompey, the servant of Major Francis Peirson, who played a decisive role in the Battle of Jersey in 1781. He is depicted firing on the French in John Singleton Copley's painting, *The Death of Major Peirson*, which hangs in the Tate Britain Gallery. People from Africa or the Caribbean came to Jersey on ships and are sometimes mentioned in the parish registers. For further information see: http://members.societe-jersiaise.org/history/niers.html.

Men born in Jersey who joined the British Army are on The National Archives website; these include Chelsea Hospital records, for example: 'WO 97/697/41 Edward Chambers, born Island of Jersey, served in 57th Foot Regiment Discharged aged 39.' There are also sailors in the Royal Navy in ADM 29/38/56. Serving and retired officers in the British Army can be found in 1828 (WO25/780-805) and in 1829 (WO25/749/79) and these have been indexed. There is a large amount of information on the officers in these records. Thomas Le Breton's career, which ended as a paymaster in 1817, is fully covered, but also included are the names and dates of birth of his children as well as dates and places of his two marriages. There is an article in the CIFHS journal no. 69 that covers these records more fully.

The Roll of Honour for the Second World War has been published and can be found in the SJL. The Passport and Identity Office (formerly the GRO) holds indexes for war deaths – 1899–1902 for Natal and South Africa, 1914–21 for the First World War and 1939–45 for the Second World War – these are for deaths that occurred outside the United Kingdom. These can be applied for through the General Register Office in Southport.

Migration

Jersey people have migrated to many countries, but it should not be forgotten that England was often the most likely destination. For example, in Poole the Durell and Mauger families settled and became involved in the cod trade, maintaining their Jersey connections. Some went to London – in the eighteenth century merchants such as Noé Le Cras or Martin de Gruchy, a notary public, were used by Jersey people as their main contact in the capital.

It was rarer for Jersey people to go to France, as anti-Protestantism would have dissuaded them. However, in 1715 Jean Martell of St Brelade went to Cognac as a wine merchant, and set up the firm that still bears his name.

Although the name of the island was given to the State of New Jersey in America, there is little evidence of emigration to that State. However, the poor were encouraged by the States of Jersey to leave the island in the late seventeenth century and go to the American colonies. Philip English, born in Trinity, Jersey in 1651, was a wealthy merchant of Salem who acted as an agent for Jersey apprentices going to America. For further details on emigrants going to America see *The Quiet Adventurers in North America* by Marion Turk.

Members of the Richardson family settled in Jamaica, and their letters have been published in the 1982 bulletin of the Société Jersiaise.

In 1848 the Church of the Latter-Day Saints, or Mormons, recruited in the island and many left to travel to Utah. The voyage of the de la Mare family was the subject of a talk to the CIFHS in 1996. The spread of Mormonism in France was undertaken by missionaries from Jersey, as they were French-speaking.

The cod banks off Newfoundland were exploited by Jerseymen from the end of the sixteenth century, but they could not settle at first. Gradually they established themselves in Newfoundland, but often came back home for the winter. For information on families in Newfoundland see: http://ngb.chebucto.org/. *Encyclopedia of Canada's Peoples*, edited by Paul R. Magocsi, also has a chapter on Channel Islanders. For further information on the Gaspé see: www.tonylesauteur.com.

The Quiet Adventurers in Canada by Marion Turk gives much interesting information on emigrants from the Channel Islands to all parts of Canada, but particularly to the Gaspé. It was here that an empire was established, that of Charles Robin, founded in 1766 with links to South America and the Mediterranean, and Jersey men were still serving with the company in the 1920s. A recent video film, *Across the Pond*, is viewable at: www.halltv.com/Across_the_Pond.html. It tells the story of Thomas Le Page, who left Jersey in 1843 to settle in the Gaspé. His house still stands, complete with its furniture, which he shipped out from Jersey.

Many of the businesses that were founded in Jersey were family enterprises, and they would often place one member of the family as their agent in another country. One member of the Lemprière family went to Faro in Portugal in the eighteenth century, probably to manage the selling of cod and maybe knitted goods; he became the British consul there. The Robin family had connections with Liverpool and the Maugers were in Poole. Thomas and Philip Morel set up Morel Bros, Shipping Company in Cardiff in 1876. Many of these families also intermarried and their business interests became entwined.

Emigration to Australia was popular from the 1850s and the first Jersey cow 'emigrated' to Australia in 1854. Although there were some ships that left from Jersey, most migrants sailed from ports in England. The *Evening*

Star, a Jersey-built ship, left the island for Australia in August 1854 with 200 Jersey, Guernsey and English people on board. There were agents in the island who advertised for migrants. *The Australian People: An Encyclopedia of the Nation, its People and their Origins*, edited by James Jupp, gives information on Channel Islanders who migrated to Australia. Despite large numbers of convicts being transported to the colony, very few of them were from Jersey. A French woman, Marie Le Gendre, who ran a brothel in St Helier was transported for the murder in 1846 of Centenier George Le Cronier (an honorary police officer).

Migration to New Zealand started from the 1840s. Early settlers may have encountered problems with the Maoris. John Gilfillan, an artist, who was born in St Brelade, went to New Zealand in 1842, but his wife and four children were killed in Whanganui in 1847; he and his surviving family then went to Australia. Emigrants could take ships from London or other ports; for example, on 13 December 1873, the *Dilharee* left Plymouth with six passengers from Jersey and nine from Guernsey; they arrived at Lyttelton on 11 March 1874. There are no combined passenger lists to New Zealand, searching has to be done through the port of entry.

The distance from Jersey was no bar to continued links with the island. Jean Helier Vautier, Mayor of Napier, New Zealand, originally from St Ouen, Jersey, went to New Zealand in 1854, but kept close contacts with Jersey. He sought brides back in the island for his sons and even sponsored six daughters of one family to come out and find husbands in New Zealand. St Helier's Bay, Auckland, was named by a Major Walmsley who had Jersey connections. For further information see: www.keithspages.com/channel.html.

On Keith Vautier's webpages (www.keithspages.com/wills.html) there is an index (incomplete) of wills that have been extracted from the first two films of probated wills recorded by the Ecclesiastical Court of Jersey (Wills and Testaments) 1660–96.

Over the centuries there have been a series of refugees: religious refugees, political refugees and those coming to seek economic opportunities. There are several important sources for French refugees in the island – both the Huguenots (Protestants) and the French Royalists – see: www.francegenweb.org/ and http://huguenots-france.org/france/poitou/poitou.htm. The journals of the Huguenot Society of London (now called the Huguenot Society of Great Britain & Ireland, www.huguenotsociety.org.uk/) are kept in the SJL, together with a list of French Protestants who were in the island in 1750. This has been reproduced in the journal of the CIFHS no. 38, spring 1988.

There are lists of French Huguenots, which includes abjurations made by the Huguenot refugees, published in the annual bulletins of the Société Jersiaise: that for 1886 covers the years 1717 to 1815, and in 1890 for 1685 to 1715; there is also a separate list of refugees who came to the island in 1750 in the SJL. An abjuration had to be made by certain Huguenots on their arrival in Jersey, as they had previously forsworn their adherence to Calvinism in France and reverted to Catholicism. Consequently, the lists are limited, but they do give details such as place of origin. The Hemerys were a Huguenot family and information on them can be found on: http://jersey familyhistory.co.uk/.

There is a microfilmed copy of a census made in 1793 of the French Royalist refugees who were then living in Jersey; the original is in The National Archives (see page 27). The list is most interesting as it gives personal details including colour of hair and eyes, height and occupation. There were more than 6,000 refugees in the island, including the writer, François René de Châteaubriand. For further information on the Royalists, reference should be made to *Les Familles Françaises à Jersey Pendant la Revolution* by R. de L'Estourbeillon. The book lists families, many of whom were aristocrats, and also a large number of Roman Catholic priests who came to Jersey. Many went on to England, but a sizeable number stayed in the island until 1815. Whilst the Royalist refugees were in the island, money was granted to them by the British Government; lists of these grants are in the Bouillon Papers (HO 69/33), which are in The National Archives. This collection is one of the largest private collections in The National Archives and consists of all the papers of Philippe d'Auvergne, Duc de Bouillon, a Jerseyman who was in charge of the Royalists during their stay in the island.

Many French people came to Jersey after 1815, particularly to work on the farms, although also as labourers and dockers. Brittany suffered from economic depression in the nineteenth century and Norman agriculture changed to dairy, which required fewer hands. In the 1900s the French who came to work in Jersey as dockers could earn three to four times what they could earn in Brittany. Marriage certificates or censuses give place of birth, which is essential in tracing French ancestors. If you have French ancestors, it is sensible to contact the relevant local genealogical society, as they are very helpful. Of particular interest is: Le Centre Généalogique des Côtes d'Armor (www.genealogie22.org/fr/), which is the genealogical society for the Départment of Côtes d'Armor (formerly Côtes du Nord), as Brittany supplied many farm workers who came from the villages near to St Brieuc. Civil registration started in 1792 and these records are online at: http://archives.cotesdarmor.fr.

The Départment of Manche, Normandy, lost many records in St Lô during the Second World War, but valiant efforts have been made to reconstitute them. Civil registrations have now been put online at: http://archives.manche.fr. Their parish registers are online at: www.pilotfamily search.org and the Cercle Généalogique de la Manche can be found at: www.cg50.org.

English people have always come to the island, sometimes as part of the garrison, and then stayed on. After 1815 many people, particularly from the south and south-west of England, came to the island in search of work. This was partly because of the agricultural depression in England and partly because of the growth of shipbuilding, building of fortifications and the opportunities for retail growth. Half-pay officers and their families, who were looking for a place to settle that had a lower cost of living than England, also came over. Greenwich pensioners were another group that settled in the island; their records are at The National Archives. The Somerset and Dorset Family History Society discovered that during the nineteenth century about 8 per cent of the population of West Dorset came to the Channel Islands.

There are no official passenger shipping lists, but the newspapers often gave the names of passengers. During the First World War, travel permits were issued and these are available at the Jersey Archive.

In the 1830s many Italians and Spaniards left their countries for political reasons – some came to Jersey and were given money by the British Government to live here; there is a list of them in the Jersey Archive, together with the amounts given to them. In 1848, the year of revolutions, the island played host to Poles, Hungarians and French refugees. The most famous Frenchman was the author, Victor Hugo, who stayed in the island for three years, 1852–55.

After the First World War colonial officers retired to the island, and after the Second World War there were many people from England who came to escape the high taxation back home.

The Jersey Archive has a large number of useful records on the registration of aliens; during the First World War the Lieutenant Governor held records on foreign nationals living in the island, which includes details of internments.

In 1920 the States of Jersey introduced the Aliens Restriction Act, which stated that all Jersey residents not of British origin over the age of 16 had to register with the immigration officer. From this process a set of cards were created with personal details such as name, address, date of birth, place of birth, movement in and out of the island and a photograph. Aliens' cards are closed for 100 years from the individual's date of birth so anyone born in 1911 or before will be available now, catalogued and indexed by name on the Jersey Archive database. An interesting example involves the registration cards belonging to Père Charles Rey: there are actually two cards for him. One was issued in 1920 when he was a student in the island at the Jesuit College at Maison St Louis (now Hotel de France). On the back of the card it says that he left for Madagascar in 1922. There is a second card for him when he arrived back in the island as a missionary in 1933. He stayed for another forty years until Highlands College closed in 1973.

It should also be noted that in the Jersey Archive is an original book for the 1901 census that has an additional column for father's birthplace for aliens.

PART THREE

Guernsey, Herm and Jethou

Chapter 9

GENERAL DESCRIPTION OF THE GEOGRAPHY, ADMINISTRATION AND HISTORY

The Bailiwick of Guernsey includes Alderney, Sark, Herm and Jethou. Guernsey, the largest island in the Bailiwick, is sixty miles from England, about twenty-six miles from Normandy, twenty-one from Jersey, twenty from Alderney and six from Sark. It is about five miles wide, north to south, by six miles from west to east.

The principal town of Guernsey is St Peter Port and there is also a small commercial port on the east coast, called St Sampson. There are ten parishes, namely: St Peter Port, St Saviour, Vale, Castel, St Sampson, St Martin, Forest, Torteval, St Peter (St Pierre du Bois) and St Andrew. These are both civil administration and ecclesiastical parishes. Perhaps because of feudal land-

Milkmaids and cows in Guernsey

holdings, the boundaries of four of the parishes are not contiguous. Torteval and St Peters bisect each other, as do Vale and St Sampsons, with a small part of Vale being on the west coast, called La Vingtaine de L'Epine. St Martins also has a small piece of land that is surrounded by the parish of Forest.

The Queen is represented by a Lieutenant Governor for the Bailiwick. The Bailiff is the highest appointed Crown officer of the Royal Court of Guernsey and the States. The Royal Court, which was established in the thirteenth century, applies a common law based on the custom of Normandy, but there are also statute laws. There are various divisions of the Royal Court, many of which have records that can be useful to family historians.

The local parliament is known as the States of Deliberation, as they were originally composed of three *États* (States), namely, the Jurats (judiciary), the Rectors (Church) and the civil administration of the parishes (the *Douzaine*). Today all members are elected as Deputies, as the role of *Conseillier* ended in 2000.

For all domestic matters the States of Deliberation makes its own laws. The *Douzaine* is the civil administrative body for the parish. There are several officials (*Douzeniers*) elected by the heads of the main families (*chefs de famille*). Each parish has two Constables, a senior one and a junior one. A representative of each *Douzaine* used to sit in the States Assembly, but have not done so since 2004. The honorary policing function ceased in 1920 when the States of Guernsey police force was established. Parishes are divided into *cantons*; usually these are numbered, but were formerly named. For example, in St Peter (St Pierre du Bois) there are four *cantons*: namely, Les Marchez, Les Yvelins, Rocquaine and Les Adams. Such names may not appear on maps, but may appear in legal or private records.

All the islands in the Bailiwick were originally a part of the Diocese of Coutances in Normandy. After the Reformation, they were transferred to the Diocese of Winchester, in Hampshire, in 1499, but this was not confirmed until about 1568. The Bishop of Winchester acts in each Deanery through a Commissary in certain local matters, particularly the Ecclesiastical Court. That Commissary is the Dean, who is known in ecclesiastical parlance as a 'peculiar'. The rectors of the parishes were ex-officio members of the States of Deliberation until 1948 and remain as members of the Electoral College that elects the Jurats. They are the lay judges of the Royal Court, who act as a permanent jury in criminal trials.

Under the parochial taxation laws of Guernsey, the rate payers are responsible for the upkeep of the church, cemetery and parsonage house. Holy Trinity, St John and St Stephen are exceptions to this system: trustees own the property, and maintain it.

The island has always been densely populated. The population of Guernsey in 1621 was estimated at 9,400 with 3,000 living in St Peter Port alone. Today the density of the island is one of the highest in Europe, with over 1,000 people per square kilometre.

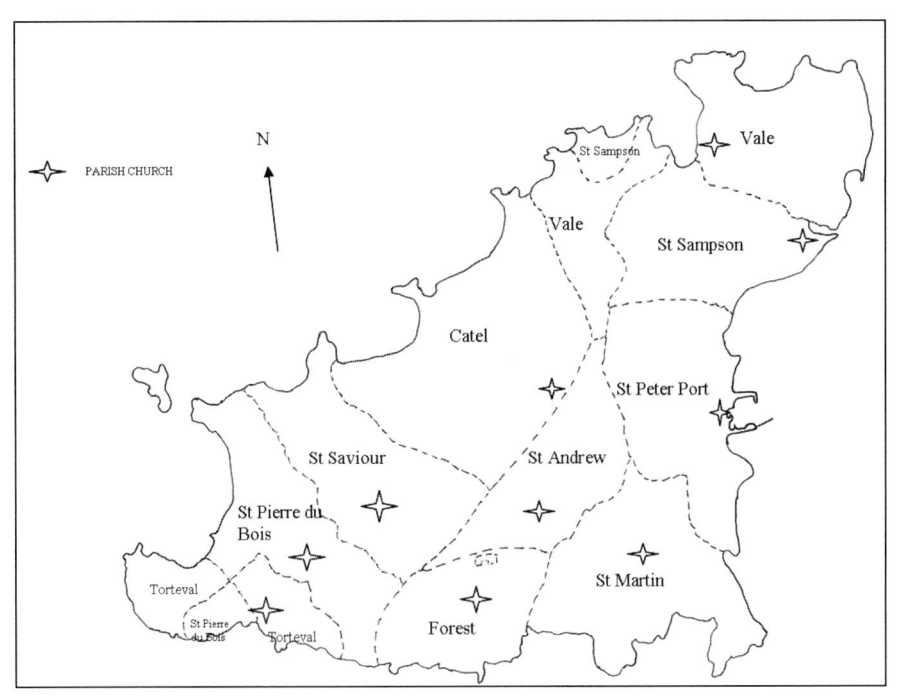

Map of the island of Guernsey, showing parish boundaries

About 9,000 years ago Guernsey became an island. The change to farming occurred in the Neolithic period about 5,000 years ago, and there are arrowheads and pottery that show early trading patterns. The island still has many dolmens, or burial mounds, which were made of large granite stones.

Roman amphorae, dating from about AD 280, were found on a wreck off St Peter Port, and indicate that the island was involved in wine trading from an early period.

Christianity came to Guernsey with Church missionaries, particularly from Wales and Brittany; one of these, St Samson, is believed to have founded a chapel about AD 560.

All the islands were attacked by Vikings and a great deal of damage was done; however, gradually the invaders settled and islanders became a part of the Duchy of Normandy, taking on the feudal system of fiefs (land holdings granted by the Duke of Normandy) with *seigneurs* (lords) owing allegiance to the Duke in return for services rendered. Guernsey was originally divided into two fiefs, although these were subsequently divided into smaller fiefs.

By the marriage of King Henry II to Eleanor of Aquitaine, the Duchy of Aquitaine became a part of the English Crown, including the important wine-producing areas around Bordeaux. When in 1204 King John lost

Normandy, the safe harbour of St Peter Port became a vital link in the export of wine from Aquitaine to England. The Papal bull of neutrality for the islands in 1481 gave a much-needed respite from French raids.

The Reformation proved a turbulent time for the islands; during the return to Catholicism during the reign of Queen Mary, three Guernsey women were accused and executed for heresy in 1556. The French Protestants, particularly from Normandy and Poitou, who were persecuted by, for example, having soldiers billeted on them, took refuge in the islands.

The English Civil War saw Guernsey taking the side of the Parliamentarians, unlike Jersey. By the end of the seventeenth century, St Peter Port had once again become an important wine entrepôt and new wealth came to the island through the activities of Guernsey privateers. Smuggling also became popular until anti-smuggling laws were passed in 1807. New trading links were made and St Peter Port became a prosperous urban centre with the New Town being built above the medieval town. Agriculture revived with the Guernsey cow, vineries and later tomatoes. Quarrying in the northern parishes provided much of the granite for London.

All the islands were occupied by the Germans from 1 July 1940 until 9 May 1945. Guernsey people were persuaded to leave the island for England – of the 42,000 inhabitants about 17,000 left, with most of the schools being evacuated – some never returned. In 1942 some English-born people were deported with those from Jersey to Germany.

After the war, agriculture and tourism gradually recovered and in the late 1960s banks and financial services developed.

A Guernsey glasshouse with vines, known as a vinery, c.1910

Herm and Jethou are both considered as a part of Guernsey. Herm, owned by the Crown but leased out, is situated to the east of Guernsey and is about a twenty-minute boat ride away. Herm, like Sark, has no cars, though tractors are used.

There is evidence of human habitation in Herm from about 10,000 BC and this continued through the Neolithic and Bronze Age periods. There are many burial chambers in the island dating from this time. Welsh monks who had settled in Sark then also went to Herm, and St Tugual was one of them; a chapel is dedicated to his name.

Herm was granted to various ecclesiastical abbeys, including Mont St Michel and a priory was established. The monks left in 1536 and the island became a hunting ground for the governors of Guernsey. Quarrying and farming came to the island in the nineteenth century, with as many as 400 men employed on the island. There were several tenants of the island and one particularly long tenancy was that of a Prussian, Prince Blücher, and his family, 1899–1916. Sir Compton Mackenzie was the next tenant of both Herm and Jethou; whilst on Herm he wrote a novel, *Fairy Gold*, based on the island. Sir Percival Perry, the next tenant, improved the island, even building a golf course. Major Peter Wood and his wife, Jenny, took on the tenancy after the Second World War and spent many happy years there, raising a family and improving facilities for tourists. The island is now tenanted by a trust company.

Jethou is privately owned and is not accessible to the public. In 1028 a Norman called Restald was given the island by Duke Robert of Normandy

The interior of St Tugual's Chapel, Herm, named after a Welsh monk who later became Bishop of Tréguier, Brittany. The chapel probably dates from 1158.

for his maritime service; he bequeathed the island to the monastery of Mont St Michel. When the alien monasteries in the islands were suppressed under Henry V in 1414 Jethou returned to the Crown. It is likely that Jethou was not inhabited, but may have been used by pirates. In 1717 Charles Nowall, from London, rented the island (and that of Herm) and built a house on Jethou. Another property seems to have been built in 1831 and at that time there were fourteen people living on the island; quarrying was carried out during this time. Various tenants held the island and one used the island as a storehouse for smuggling brandy. In 1920 Sir Compton Mackenzie, the writer, leased the island, restored the house and added a new wing, although he and his wife left in 1934. From 1964 until 1971 the Faed family lived there and Susan Faed has written about the island.

In 1971 the late Sir Charles Hayward took over the lease and made further alterations to the house. The present tenant is Sir Peter Ogden.

Lihou is a small island off the west coast of Guernsey, which is connected to the mainland at low tide. There was a small priory dedicated to St Mary and a house, which has been reconstructed.

Chapter 10

CIVIL RECORDS AND CENSUSES

Civil registration started in 1840 and the records are kept by the Royal Court. The Guernsey registrar is Her Majesty's Greffier (see Directory). There is a separate alphabetical index, which is continuous to the present day, so searching is very quick. The Priaulx Library also has the indices on microfilm. Copies of the Church of England marriages were not sent to the Greffe until 1919, so if searching for a marriage before then, it is best to start with the parish registers.

Unlike English certificates death certificates in Guernsey are particularly useful, as they give the names of the parents of the deceased and the place of birth.

Birth certificates give the parish of birth, date of birth, name of child, name of father and name of mother before marriage, where born, rank or profession of father and date of registration.

Marriage certificates give the date of marriage, the Christian names and surnames of the couple, their ages, their condition (i.e. bachelor, spinster, widow, widower or divorced), their rank, state or profession, their residence, their father's name and his rank, state or profession, the couple's signatures together with the place of marriage and the parish, and the signatures of the two witnesses.

The death certificate gives the date and hour of death, the name and surname (in the case of women who have been married, their maiden surname and name of their husband and their condition), their age, the name of the father and mother (and her maiden name), where they died, rank or profession and usual abode, where born, certified cause of death, date of registration, and by whom the death was registered.

Although registration was supposed to be comprehensive, recent research by Rose-Marie Crossan (in her book, *Guernsey 1814–1914: Migration and Modernisation*) has shown that the number of births registered was significantly lower than the number of baptisms, even though non-registration incurred a fine. It is suggested that some religious groups had objections to registration. So it is important to look in the baptism registers from 1840 until probably the beginning of the 1890s. Curiously, the under-registration seems to apply to deaths as well. The under-registration of births may be as high as

Island of Guernsey

No. 19154

Certified Copy of an Entry of Death in the Island of Guernsey

No.	Date and Hour of Death	Name and Surname	Age	Name of Father and Mother (Maiden name)	Where died	Rank, or Profession and usual abode	Where Born	Certified Cause of Death	When Registered
1	1909 January first 4:00 a.m.	Mary Mahon widow of James Henry	89	Daniel Mahon Judith Ogier	Wanbrook Cottage, Brock Road, S:Peter Port	— Brock Road, S:Peter Port, Guernsey	S:Peter Port, Guernsey	paralysis Dr. Corbin	1909 January second

I certify the above to be true copy of an entry in the General Register of Deaths in the Island of Guernsey.

Registrar-General's Office, Guernsey, this 30d. day of December 20 04

Deputy Registrar-General.

Death certificate from Guernsey, which gives the name of the deceased's parents and the deceased's place of birth

40 per cent, but for deaths it was even higher at 50 per cent. Death registration appears to have improved after the opening of the Foulon Cemetery in 1856.

Stillbirths have been registered since the year 2000 and are only registered if occurring after twenty-four weeks of pregnancy.

Microfilm copies of the indexes to the births, marriages and deaths were made by the Mormons and are available at their centres. A copy is also held at the Society of Genealogists in London.

Certificates of births, marriages and deaths relating to Guernsey people in England during the Second World War include their Guernsey addresses in the occupation column, and copies are held in the Island Archives. There is also a microfilm copy in the Society of Genealogists.

The Channel Islands refugees in England during the Second World War published magazines, such as the *Stockport and District Channel Islands Society Monthly Review*, which recorded births, marriages and deaths in England; these can be found in the SJL, together with an index, and the Priaulx Library. Exceptionally, there are double registrations that are kept outside the island; these are for military families garrisoned in the island and for French nationals. (It is possible that other nationalities can also register with their consul, but this has not been checked.)

The regimental returns (also called Chaplains' Returns, Army returns, etc.) for baptisms, births, marriages and deaths cover 1761 (for baptisms) until 1924; marriages date from 1796. For example, George Dorr was baptised in Guernsey in 1815; his father belonged to the 87th Regiment. The indexes for these are available at The National Archives and copies of the entries can be obtained from the General Registrar's Office in Southport. There are also separate registers for births and deaths at sea.

French nationals registered births in Guernsey with the French consul and these records are now kept in Nantes in the Archives Diplomatiques de France.

Adoption was legal in Guernsey from 1935. Those who wish to access original birth records should first contact the Birth Records Counsellor at Perruque House, Rue de la Perruque, Castel, Guernsey.

The Registrar at the Greffe keeps records of any contact or request for information in the files and if a contact from a birth parent matches with one from the adopted adult or vice versa, the Registrar will act as intermediary and put the two parties in touch with each other.

There are websites that allow people searching for natural parents or their adopted children to post information on them; for example, there is a Channel Islands section on the Adoption Registry Connect website: www.adopteeconnect.com.

Censuses

As for Jersey, there was no census taken in 1801 or 1811; the first two are for 1821 and 1831, both of which only contain information in terms of numbers.

The number of inhabitants can vary according to the date of the census – they might, for example, include tourists or farm workers, which might outweigh the sailors who were away. In some years the sailors were enumerated on their ships in ports in the British Isles, but those who were at sea or in foreign ports would not, of course, be included.

The totals for the Bailiwick (i.e. including Alderney, Sark, Herm and Jethou) are: 1821, 20,827; 1831, 26,128; 1841, 28,521; 1851, 33,719; 1861, 35,365; 1871, 33,969; 1881, 35,257; 1891, 35,287; 1901, 40,446; 1911, 41,858; 1921, 38,315; 1931, 40,643; 1951, 43,652; 1961, 45,068; 1981, 53,313; 1991, 58,867; 2001, 59,807; 2008, 61,726.

In 1821 Herm had a population of 28, but when the quarrying started the 1831 census shows an enormous increase to 177 people. Life returned to a more normal level and in 1841 there were 38 people living there; in 1851 it was 46 and in 1861 it had slightly shrunk to 41. In 1871 Herm had a population of 83, which went down to 20 in 1881. The following censuses showed a little growth: 1891, 38; 1901, 25; 1911, 33; 1921, 32; 1931, 53.

Jethou also had a higher population in 1831, up to fourteen, which was five more than in 1821. The population then remained constant at six for 1841, three in 1851, five in 1861 and four for 1871 and 1881. There were six in 1891, three in 1901, only two in 1911 and none in 1921, although it returned to two in 1931.

The major genealogical companies now have all the censuses for the Bailiwick of Guernsey; the 1881 census is freely available on: www.familysearch.org and through the LDS family history centres worldwide. There are some records on the Free Census website: www.freecen.org.uk.

The 1911 census should become more available shortly and there are moves to release the 1921 census ahead of 2022. The census returns for 1931 were all destroyed in 1942.

There are some problems associated with transcriptions, so it is advisable to use the locally created indexes. Some were compiled and co-ordinated by Mr and Mrs R.J. Morgan, whilst others were indexed by members of the Family History Section of La Société Guernesiaise. These indexes are being re-checked for accuracy by the Priaulx Library.

Unpublished typed indexes for 1841, 1851, 1861, 1881, 1891 and 1901 (which include the islands of Alderney, Sark, Herm and Jethou) are presently available in the Channel Islands, either at the Priaulx Library and at the archive room of the the Family History Section of La Société Guernesiaise in Guernsey; as well as in Jersey at the SJL and in the CIFHS research collection at Jersey Archive. Copies are also available at the Society of Genealogists. Lorna Pratt notes in her transcript of the 1841 census (www.members.shaw.ca/jerseymaid/Guernseymain.html) that some women were enumerated under their maiden names.

The Island Archives hold the identity registration cards created during the German Occupation, giving details of all islanders over 14 who stayed in the island, and there are photographs on many of the cards. There is a separate set of cards for those who died during the Occupation. There are also some forms for those who returned after the liberation in May 1945.

In the Island Archives there are fragments of the census for the parish of Vale for 1821. The 1827 census for St Pierre du Bois and for St Peter Port (see: http://user.itl.net/~glen/constables.html) is in the Island Archives and the Priaulx Library has a microfilm of this. Also in the Island Archives is a register of all passengers landing in the island from 1828 to 1832. On 20 August 1827, in the presence of the Bailiff, Daniel de Lisle Brock, an extraordinary assembly of the Royal Court was called 'as a consequence of recent thefts and attempted thefts on the public highways, and the danger to life from firearms used in break ins and general complaints received about the great number of suspicious strangers walking about in the town and the country, many without anywhere to live'. There were also other complaints about 'colporteurs', nineteenth-century travelling salesmen who, on the pretext of offering their merchandise, were getting into private homes and gathering information that was assumed would be used for future burglaries. The Royal Court decided that action was required and took the following steps:

St Sampson's Harbour, Guernsey. Ships here were chiefly involved in the export of granite.

1. All persons occupying houses, or part of a house, within eight days after the publication of the present order, should give to the Constables of their respective parishes a list of all those who occupy that house, or part of a house.
2. This list should distinguish between Natives and non-Natives and children who are under age, those born in the Island must be on the same list as their fathers.
3. Any changes to the list must be reported within 24 hours. If someone leaves and another moves in, the owner of the house must inform the Constables. Those who do not adhere to these three clauses can be fined an amount not exceeding 50 Livres Tournois.
4. The Constables of the Parishes will keep a book and go to each house, with the list, to check that it is correct. The Constables will keep another book for the non-natives only, strangers who have been living in the parish more than a month, and another for strangers who have lived there less than one month. After they have lived there for that month their names should be transferred to the first list. All changes to the list must be reported to the Constables and entered into the books with dates of the report.
5. All the Masters of Vessels, Barques or Boats arriving on this Island, must provide on their arrival, or after 24 hours at the latest, the Constables with an exact list of all passengers who have disembarked. [Failure carried the penalty of a 70 Livres Tournois fine per passenger disembarked, who had not been reported.]
6. It is forbidden to anybody, after the publication of the present law, to sell merchandise on the roads and public highways or to offer to sell on the roads, houses or anywhere else, if they do not have a place to sell these items. They can sell from premises, but those who break the law will be liable to a fine not exceeding 50 Livres Tournois. Despite this order it is possible for reputable tradesmen who wish to sell to ask permission from the Constable, but no further trading in the roads will be allowed. This law will be presented in public and published so that no one can plead ignorance.

The first set of records are organised by *Vingtaine* (district), beginning with Vingtaine de la Grand Rue, then the Pollet, etc., and contain the following three headings: 'Natives or Spouses of Natives who are Permanently Established', 'Strangers who Intend to Stay at a House or Lodgings of their Own' and 'Those Passing Through, Resident at Hotels or Other Lodgings for Strangers'. Beneath each column males and females are separately listed and grouped together by household. The houses are not named, but listed by the name of the owner (e.g. Edouard Brouard's). Children are counted, but not named. All the non-natives of Guernsey during this period of the nineteenth century are here. After the statistics comes an indexed list of male strangers (abstracted from the main list), each of whom has been allocated a number, making them easy to locate.

An entry looks like this: 'NAME: Thos. Coke Isham (wife and child) AGE: 22 COUNTY OF ORIGIN: Antigua WHERE RESIDENT: At Mrs Baxter's, High Street PROFESSION: Plasterer LENGTH OF RESIDENCE: 6 years.' Going on to the register of passengers landed, this book is not indexed and contains five columns headed: list of passengers, where from, date, profession, ship's master and port (of departure).

Also among the Constables' records are two stranger poor lists, one from 1848, which is indexed and the other from 1892, which also contains the Constable's record of funds used to send them home – in some cases back to England. Householders and strangers' censuses for 1827 for St Martin and St Pierre du Bois have also survived and are in the custody of the Island Archives.

Chapter 11

CHURCH REGISTERS, NAMES AND CEMETERIES

There are ten parishes in Guernsey, each with its own Church of England parish church, but there are only eight rectors, as Vale is combined with St Sampson and Forest with Torteval (since at least 1833). The parishes of St Pierre du Bois, Torteval, Forest, St Saviour, St Andrew and St Martin are known as *les hautes paroisses* (the higher parishes) and St Peter Port, St Sampson, Castel and Vale are known as *les basses paroisses* (the lower parishes).

The parish registers for St Peter Port, Vale, and St Andrew, and the church registers for St John, St Barnabus and St James are kept at the Priaulx Library; all the other registers are kept by the Rectors or are in the Island Archives.

Parish	Baptisms	Marriages	Burials
St Peter Port (St Pierre du Port/ Town Church)	1563	1565	1566
Vale (St Michel du Valle)	1577	1577	1577
St Peter (St Pierre du Bois)	1625	1625	1625
Castel (Notre Dame de la Delivrance de Castel, or Ste Marie du Castel)	1674	1674	1674
St Sampson	1713	1713	1713
St Saviour (St Sauveur)	1582	1582	1609
St Martin (St Martin de la Bellouse)	1660	1660	1728
Forest (Ste Marguerite de la Forêt)	1700	1700	1704
St Andrew (St André de la Pommeraye)	1575	1573	1574
Torteval (St Philippe de Torteval)	1684	1721	1739

All the Church of England parish registers have been microfilmed and these are in the Priaulx Library. Copies of entries can be supplied at £1 each, but please note that the copyright is vested with the Rectors, so the records should not be published in books or on the Internet. All the registers have been indexed, some by members of the Family History Section of La Société Guernesiaise. Some have been also been transcribed, but they may not be complete.

There are, of course, gaps as well as omissions in the registers. St Andrew, for example, has gaps for 1599–1603 and 1616–19.

In the early nineteenth century the population of St Peter Port increased so much that four ecclesiastical districts were created; copies of the following registers are in the Priaulx Library:

St John the Evangelist: baptisms from 1840 to 1869, marriages 1858–1974; St Stephen: baptisms 1865–1965, marriages 1885–1986 and burials 1885–1957; Holy Trinity: baptisms 1847–1988, marriages 1858–1988, burials 1858–1988; St Paul (demolished 1971): baptisms 1841–1935, marriages 1923–36; and St Barnabas: baptisms 1881–1913.

Holy Trinity Church, St Peter Port, was a Methodist church and registers from 1787 are in the Island Archives; it then became a Church of England church from 1846. The church of St James-the-Less was the garrison church, built in 1818 to provide services in English and there is a marriage register 1915–70 in the Priaulx Library, with records also in the Island Archives.

St Matthew, Cobo, Castel, was built after an initiative started by Marianne Carey, who was concerned that the families of fishermen had too far to walk to the parish church. The Priaulx Library has baptism records from 1854 onwards and marriages and burials from 1855; see: www.guernsey.net/~st-matthews.

There is also a garrison register kept by the chaplain for the soldiers mainly at Fort George; the Priaulx Library has a copy of the baptisms and burials for 1794–1810.

The notebook of Pierre Le Roy (1600–1675), who was schoolmaster of St

The Parish Church of St Michel du Valle dates from about 1155. This part of the Vale parish was originally a separate island until 1806 when the Braye du Valle was filled in; parishioners would have had to row across at high tide in order to attend services.

Martin, contains interesting family material that may well be typical of the experiences of other Guernsey families – children died young, wives died in childbirth, and men remarried, creating a complex network of family relationships. A translated extract shows the detail he described:

> I, Peter le Roy, son of Peter, and Anne Brett, my wife, were married on the 15th Day of the month of November, 1617 in the Church of St Sampson, by Master Thomas Millet, minister of the said Church. My sister, Rachel le Roy, was married to Thomas Doré on the 25th of November, 1613. And at that time I was in England to learn the language, and lived first at Wareham and afterwards at Poole . . . Ursula, our first born, was baptized on the 8th of August, in the year 1619, and presented by my father-in-law, John Wright, who at that time was a soldier at Castle Cornet, and had married my wife's mother, Ursula de Vick, as her second husband, after the decease of Edmund Brett, her first husband, my wife's father, who then was Captain in one of the ships of the late Queen Elizabeth of happy memory, and he died and two of his sons with him on the coast of Spain. The ship split asunder under their feet. The said Ursula, our first born, died about 40 days after her baptism.

Between 1620 and 1646 Pierre and Anne had ten further children, with eight surviving childhood. Pierre records other events in the notebook:

> Saturday, December 17, 1659. My son-in-law Anthony Breton's house was robbed, and a case was taken from my daughter's coffer, in which there were two gold rings and an embroidered girdle, two silver pins and her husband's wedding stockings which were dyed scarlet in grain and were worth a crown or more, and the girdle was worth a pistole of 10 livres tournois.

Their youngest son, Josué, was not fortunate with his wives; he married Marie Mansell in 1668 and she died in 1686; he married his second wife, Elizabeth Allées in 1687, and

> I let my house at Les Landes to go and live with her on her farm. She died on Wednesday, the 23rd of January, 1688, being near her confinement. God keep all good people from falling into such trouble as I am now in by the death of these two poor creatures, whose deaths have often made me long for my own.

He may have hoped that his luck had changed when he married Rachel Mauger in July 1689: although they had a son, their second child, a daughter – Rachel, born 25 December 1691 – died only two hours after her birth as a result of Josué and Rachel having been assaulted by soldiers.

Marriages recorded in St Peter Port in the last years of the eighteenth century show a wide variety of countries from which the participants came: several New Yorkers, for example, were married there. In 1796 places of origin included Holstein, Germany, Cowhorse Bay, Massachusetts, Gibraltar, Quebec, Amsterdam and Norway. Some records give the father's name, but this is unusual until the 1820s. Many people from the other islands were married in Guernsey, particularly St Peter Port; St Andrew's Church was popular for fashionable weddings. As in Jersey, Guernsey appears to have been used as a kind of Gretna Green in the eighteenth and nineteenth centuries, especially for those living in the south of England. After Lord Hardwicke's Act of 1754, which did not allow minors to marry without parental consent, advertisements were placed in the newspapers in the south coast of England advising of the availability of boats to bring the eloping couple across the Channel. In a similar way the Channel Islands were used when a widower wished to marry his dead wife's sister, as this was forbidden by English Canon Law, but not by the Canon Laws of the Channel Islands.

Dower rights were an important part of island life. Marie de Garis suggested that the bride's family would provide furniture for the couple as her dowry, with the husband's providing the marriage bed. The bride's family might also contribute a milch cow with a calf. A widow was usually entitled to a third of her husband's property, and a widower to a life interest in his wife's property; such rights depended on whether the property was inherited or acquired. The laws were based on Norman succession laws.

As in Jersey, godparents played an important role and, as they were often relatives, they should not be ignored. Although Calvinism imposed rigidity on Guernsey society, weddings and funerals were opportunities for festivity. The coming of Methodism meant a return to the earlier sobriety. Marie de Garis wrote thus about funerals:

> True, the ritual and ostentatiousness of the burying of the dead remained. The slow, silent walking procession to the Churchyard, led by the pastor, every house on the route with drawn blinds, the 'funeral' bell tolling mournfully as the procession approached, the black habits, the taking of mourning in the deceased's pew the following Sunday, these remained. But the ham, the 'houichepottes' and, above all, the drinking on returning home after the burial, these were gone. Instead, the mourners sat down in the darkened room to a quiet repast of dry bread and cheese.

Church pews were owned, usually, in right of property. In some instances, men and women were separated in the church. In 1710 in the church of St Pierre du Bois there is a seating plan that mentions *le premier Banc à fêmmes* (the first women's pew).

Roman Catholic and Non-Conformist Registers

After the Protestant Reformation, the island became a Calvinist stronghold and later was part of the Church of England. When the French Revolution

French stone crackers at a quarry in St Sampson, Guernsey, c.1905

came, and with it the oath of allegiance required of priests to the Republic, many French Catholic clergy fled to the island. Priests were permanently in the island from 1802 onwards and in 1829 a chapel was built on the site of Notre Dame in Burnt Lane, St Peter Port. The foundation stone of St Joseph's Church was laid on 21 May 1846, only a short time after the land at Cordier Hill had been secured for a new church. Cardinal Wiseman, Archbishop of Westminster, opened St Joseph, designed by Augustus Welby Pugin, in 1851. The name of Mary, wife of Joseph, was added to retain the title of the chapel at Burnt Lane, which had been closed at the opening of St Joseph in 1851. Notre Dame re-opened in 1860 to serve the French-speaking community, and Our Lady, Star of the Sea, at St Sampson was built in 1879 to serve the Irish community who worked in the granite quarries.

In 1882 the Channel Islands became part of the Diocese of Portsmouth, a link that still remains.

Only Notre Dame, St Joseph and St Mary and Our Lady, Star of the Sea remain open; the other chapels have closed.

The following Roman Catholic registers are available at the Priaulx Library:

	Baptisms	Marriages	Burials
Notre Dame du Rosaire, St Peter Port	1802–1991	1802–1991	1802–1985
St Joseph and St Mary, St Peter Port	1850–1990	1856–1974	1856–1976
Our Lady, Star of the Sea, St Sampson	1897–1996	1952–1994	1952–1996
La Chaumière, Castel	1850–1990	1856–1974	1856–1976
St Magloire, Vale	1897–1923		
St Yves, Forest	1904–1990	1936–1985	1905–1984

Methodism came to Guernsey in 1783; there are two circuits, English and French. The first chapel was built in Rue Le Marchant, St Peter Port, in 1788 and was the first in the Channel Islands.

The Priaulx Library has the following records:

	Baptisms	Marriages	Burials
Bordeaux, Vale		1926–1945	
Ebenezer, Brock Road, St Peter Port		1880–1955	
Delancey, St Sampson	1866–1933		
Delisle, Castel		1919–1927	
Ebenezer, Union Street, St Peter Port		1898–1959	
Forest	1906–1959		
French Circuit	1885–1934		
Galaad, Castel		1926–1951	
L'Islet	1938–1979	1938–1979	
Methodist New Connexion		1837–1841	
Morley		1898–1939	
Rohais, St Andrew's	1919–1928		
St Andrew's	1919–1988		
St Martin's	1906–1922	1919–1984	1885–1898
St Martin's Mission	1906–1992	1931–1974	
St Paul's, Vale	1841–1935	1923–1936	
St Sampson's	1866–1958	1866–1980	
St Peter's, Sion	1903–1962	1912–1950	1904–1957
Truchot	1874–1933		
Vale	1907–1989	1919–1982	
Victoria Road		1919–1982	
Wesleyan		1841–1863	

The Ebenezer Church in Union Street was built in 1815; in 1834 a panic, after gas lights flickered, resulted in a crush that killed six young women and girls and a boy of 12. The church was sold in 1960 and the Brock Road Methodist Church took on the name of Ebenezer.

Copies of other church registers that are also in the Priaulx Library include: the two chapels for the Independents, La Chapelle Independante Française (baptisms 1841–73) and L'Église Independante (baptisms 1821–42); the Eldad Elim Church in St Peter Port (baptisms 1841–1985); Salem Baptist (1839–41); and St Saviour's Independent (baptisms 1841–1927). The baptism records of Siloe, Bethesda and Bethel (which are now all Shiloh) are in the Island Archives.

There is a United Reformed Church in St Saviour; St Andrew in the Grange, built in 1897, belongs to the Church of Scotland – for further information see: www.cofsguernsey.org.gg/history.html. The Society of Friends (Quakers), established in 1782 in Guernsey, has a meeting room in St Peter Port.

Cemeteries

There are churchyards around all the parish churches in Guernsey, but the cemetery adjacent to the town church in St Peter Port became unusable by the 1780s; this was known as the Sisters' Cemetery (*Les Soeurs*). Alternative sites were used: there was the Brothers' Cemetery (*Les Frères*), originally established about 1670 probably near where the Franciscan friars lived and the Strangers' Cemetery (*Le Cimetère des Estrangers*), started in 1780, which was used by the garrison as well as for strangers and paupers. It become full by 1857 and closed in 1928, the site being cleared in the 1970s. The Candie Cemetery was then built in the 1830s. The Foulon cemetery in Vale was opened in 1856 and the records include both burials and cremations.

The burial records for the following cemeteries are available at the Priaulx Library: The Brothers' Cemetery 1847–1930, Candie Cemetery 1831–1986, Foulon Cemetery 1856–1991, the Vale Independent Cemetery 1881–1988 and the Strangers' Cemetery 1847–73. The monumental inscriptions for the Plymouth Brethren (a movement of Evangelical Christians, founded in Dublin in the late 1820s) have also been collated. Burial registers of Foulon (1856–1963), Vale (1883–1995), and St Martin (1904 onwards) are in the Island Archives, and there is a list of the Candie Cemetery records (1831–2004) by Gillian Lenfestey. The Strangers' Cemetery (1780–1880) in St Peter Port has also been indexed by surname, the Reverend Carey having taken notes of many of the gravestones in 1933; it is online at: www.genealogy.guernsey.net/Stranger.html.

David Kreckeler has published an index to the Brothers' Cemetery, 1719–1948. The work was undertaken by a small band of dedicated volunteers from the Family History Section of La Société Guernesiaise and the records are also in their research room. There are several churchyards where

Anchor on the grave of a mariner, St Andrew's Church, Guernsey. Other gravestones have ships engraved upon them.

the monumental inscriptions have already been fully transcribed – St Pierre du Bois, Castel, St Andrew, St Matthew (Castel) and St John (St Peter Port) – and are at the Priaulx Library.

For the garrison cemetery and Fort George war memorials, see: www.greatwarci.net/memorials/guernsey/guernsey-memorials.htm and www.adaswar.net/memorials/ci-mems/ci-memorials-gu-list.htm, showing inscriptions and photographs. There is a war memorial to dead Guernseymen who were killed in the South African wars at the bottom of St Julian's Avenue. The journal of the CIFHS publishes from time to time a strays' list of those from the Channel Islands who have been buried abroad. Extracts have also been made of notices from newspapers of those who died abroad; enquiries should be made to the Strays Coordinator, c/o The Channel Islands Family History Society.

A crematorium was built at the Foulon Cemetery in 1929, which was a comparatively early date for crematoriums. Those who have died in Alderney, Sark, Herm or Jethou and wished their bodies to be cremated were transported to Guernsey.

Surnames and Christian Names

Some typical Guernsey surnames include: Allez, Brock, de la Rue, de Jersey (indicating that the family originated in Jersey – although there does not appear to be a similar 'de Guernsey' family in Jersey), de Garis and Falla (originating from Gascony), Le Patourel, Le Mesurier and Lenfestey. The de Saumarez, Andros and Carey families were well established and provided the island with many officials, such as Bailiffs and Jurats. Surnames that have been researched by the Priaulx Library are on the resource list page: www.priaulxlibrary.co.uk/downloads.asp#resourcelist.

On the website for the Guernsey Society there is a useful article on surnames, see: www.guernsey-society.org.uk/famhist.htm – this also gives links to some useful websites on Guernsey families, including those of the Le Mesuriers, Thoumine, Carey and Renouf families.

Although women were legally always known by their maiden names, quite often they would be described colloquially as, for example, 'Rachel, *femme de* (wife of) Nicolas Lihou', without mentioning her maiden name.

The Church had a major influence on the naming of children and the late sixteenth-century ordinances meant that Christian names became less varied than before. In the Carey family, for example, there were male names with feminine diminutives such as Jenette, Collette, Guillemette and Thomasse. Some Christian names such as André and Elizée (male name) were popular in Guernsey, but appear rarely in the other islands.

In Guernsey women were also permitted to present children for baptism as well as men, differing from the practice in Jersey. Godparents also had to be over the age of 14.

Chapter 12

PROPERTY AND OFFICIAL RECORDS

The *Guernsey House* by John McCormack gives detailed information on houses in the island dating from before 1787. It also includes details of family ownership and gives a good background to the way of life in Guernsey. The map of 1787 by William Gardner is provided in the book, which shows all the houses in the island at that time.

Alex Glendinning has noted some datestones, many with photographs, on: http://members.societe-jersiaise.org/alexgle/stonegsy.html. Sometimes these commemorate a marriage, but more usually the date relates to changes in the property. As in Jersey, the initials are syllabic: NFL, for instance, represents Nicolas Falla. There are some marks of merchants on buildings in St Peter Port. For architectural and historical information on St Peter Port, *Buildings in the Town and Parish of St Peter Port* by C. Brett is invaluable.

Almanacs and directories that date from the late eighteenth century give lists of inhabitants and their addresses; these can be found in the Priaulx Library. Telephone books can also give addresses. The Royal Court of Guernsey has a large number of records that are in the care of the Greffe, including property transactions (*contrats*), which are known as *Date* (spoken – but copied out) and *Lire* (written), but these were combined in 1922. These are the contracts that are presented before the Royal Court and registered. They date from 1576 and were in French until 1969; they are indexed both by the surname of the vendor (*bailleur*) and the purchaser (*acquéreur*). Unusually there are also contracts that register land in Canada owned by Guernsey people.

There are many plans of conveyances, particularly from 1900. For further information on them, it is best to approach the archivists at the Island Archives who can provide guidance. The records also contain many maps of properties. Note that married women are usually referred to by their maiden names. Some marriage contracts were registered in the Royal Court, others may be in private collections. The main reason for a contract was to ensure that the wife's own property remained hers in the event of her husband becoming bankrupt, or to return her property (or his) to the respective family if they had no children. There were, however, dower rights for both widower and widow.

Une vieille cuisine *(an old kitchen), Guernsey. This postcard shows a typical interior with a 'Welsh' wicker chair, with the* jonchière *(green bed) to the right of the fireplace.*

Wills of realty (real property, i.e. houses and land) were permitted from 1841. Prior to that there were strict rules of succession, according to Norman customary laws. These wills have to be registered in the Royal Court and can be found in the Greffe, with a large card index for them.

From 1982, property records are at the Cadastre Department, La Ramée, St Peter Port. The records are indexed by the name of the property, and include details of the owners. This department is very busy, dealing with rating matters and rent control, and has little time to undertake research requests. Copies can, however, be provided. If visiting in person, make an appointment (01481 721239). From 2007 there has been a tax on property and land. The Cadastre also deals with property in Alderney.

For maps of modern Guernsey, see the Guernsey Digimap: http://maps.digimap.gg/. There are several different viewing options, including population density and road names, but access to the Cadastre is restricted.

Livres de perchage are manuscripts and published records of land ownership of the fiefs dating from the fifteenth century, although most are from the late eighteenth century. There are *livres* for the Crown fief, but there are some areas, such as reclaimed land, which do not belong to a fief and are therefore *non en perchage*. They list the landowners together with the names of the property, the fields and their area. Although some remain in private hands many are kept at the Priaulx Library, while others are in the Island Archives and the Greffe. For further information see: http://user.itl.net/~glen/livresdesperchages.html and www.priaulxlibrary.co.uk/images/library/LivresdePerchage.pdf.

There are records in the Island Archives that give details of the Channel Islands (property) rehabilitation scheme that operated after the German Occupation and gave compensation for damage to islanders' property. For insurance records see Sun Fire Insurance records, which were formerly at the London Guildhall (www.history.ac.uk/gh/fire.htm); they are now available on The National Archives website.

Information on property ownership is also available in the rating lists for the parishes, which are kept with the individual parishes. For example, in St Pierre du Bois in 1729 the parish had seventy-two ratepayers and a total of 1,500 *livres tournois* was raised. Jean Allès of La Tourelle was the richest man in the parish and paid 107 *livres tournois.* Inventories can also be useful and interesting: Judith Le Messurier, of St Pierre du Bois, who died in 1753, left a horse and a pig, as well as her red petticoat. Such inventories can be found in private records as well as parish ones.

The Royal Court records include those for inheritance, bankruptcy, inquests and many other items. Records of deed polls date from 1947. The Acts of the Royal Court are known as *ordonnances* and those for 1533–1840 have been published. The Acts of the States, *Actes des États*, have also been published for 1605–1845.

Ecclesiastical Court

The wills of personalty are proved by the Ecclesiastical Court and the records are kept by them. However, each book is indexed individually and these are kept by the Greffe. Permission must be sought from the Ecclesiastical Court before copies can be made, and the Greffier can do this for you. The wills of the Ecclesiastical Court are on microfilm with indexes for 1664–1899; they are in the Priaulx Library. It should be noted that contrary to succession laws and wills of realty the eldest son did not get *préciput* in the area of St Peter Port that was bounded by the *barrières de la ville* (town barriers), but this has now been abolished.

Guernsey people who had property in England appear in The National Archives for the Prerogative Court of Canterbury 1384–1858 and the wills are available through their DocumentsOnline service. After that date the wills are in the Probate Registry in London (First Avenue House, High Holborn, London, WC1V 6NP); the indexes 1861–1941 are now searchable on the Ancestry website. There are over 2,000 references to Guernsey people on this.

All the churches have their own records and some of these are with the Priaulx Library; for example, there are confirmation registers 1882–1922 for St James, which are available on microfilm.

The Ecclesiastical Court had wide-ranging powers that regulated much of Guernsey's life. They were particularly concerned with the behaviour of young people and strangers.

Parochial Records

The Constables' Office in St Peter Port had a wide range of documents, which have been deposited with the Island Archives. These include tax records from 1740, lists of passengers landed 1828–32 and the census of 1827. The records from other parishes are also held by the Island Archives.

Electoral lists are not published but one can check them at the *Douzaine* office for each parish. The age of majority in Guernsey was 20, but since 1978 it has been 18.

Earlier Records

There were originally two fiefs in Guernsey, that of the Fief du Bessin and the Fief du Cotentin; then there was a lot of subdivision, so that there are about seventy today. See: www.morhov.or/Guernsey-pht-2.htm. All *seigneural* dues were abolished in 1980. The *Livres de Perchages*, which are held in the Greffe, the Priaulx Library and the Island Archives, are invaluable and the earliest date from the late 1400s. The Crown fief records are known as *Extentes* and these have been published; the earliest starts in 1274.

The assize rolls are also available for 1299 and 1309; originally in Latin, there is a full translation into English. These are full of interesting material and include an index by names. Although primarily concerned with criminal acts, there are also mentions of accidents; for example, in the parish of Vale 'when John Graydon was working in a quarry with a certain pickaxe stones fell upon him whereupon he died immediately and nobody else is suspected.' Sometimes the instrument of death was forfeited: in this incident, the pickaxe. Another case in the Vale parish concerned Geoffrey le (sic) Cu who 'moved by poverty and grief hanged himself'.

Chapter 13

EDUCATION, EMPLOYMENT AND CRIME

Education

Following the Reformation, schools were established in the parishes, with teaching provided either by the rector or by the appointed schoolmaster. Often the schoolroom was in the church, though sometimes schooling took place in a room in a house or in a purpose-built property. In St Pierre du Bois the parish school was provided with an annual wheat *rente* in 1568 and appears to have been in a separate building. This fell into a poor state by 1759 and although there were problems, eventually a new school was built by 1766.

School hours were from 9 a.m. to 12 p.m. and 1 p.m. until 3 p.m. in the winter, with longer hours in the summer (8 a.m.–12 p.m. and 1 p.m.–4 p.m.). The holidays were for twelve days over Christmas, four weeks during August and two weeks in the autumn and the spring so that the children could help with the gathering of *vraic* (seaweed used as a fertiliser). A school for girls was not opened until 1814.

Parish schools were started in St Peter Port, and St Martin in the sixteenth century. In 1563 a grammar school was founded and named after Queen Elizabeth I; it was situated at the top of St Peter Port, near to where it stands today. However, by the end of the eighteenth century it had only a few pupils. Sir John Colbourne, the Lieutenant Governor, ordered a public inquiry into education at the college, which resulted in the construction of a new building – this is still the main college building today. The college re-opened in 1824 with English tutors being employed. The school publishes registers of pupils and those for 1824–1977 are available at the Priaulx Library; they contain helpful biographical details of former pupils.

Children might be sent to schools in England or to French academies. Guernsey boys tended to go to the University of Cambridge and the records for Oxford (1500–1886) and Cambridge (1261–1900) are available either in libraries or on the Ancestry website; there are 217 references to Guernsey in the Cambridge records – although the place of birth is not given, there are references to addresses and schooling in the island.

Today most of the parishes have a States' primary school and there are some private ones, as well as States' and private secondary schools.

Elizabeth College, St Peter Port, Guernsey, built in 1826–29, and shown on this postcard as it was in about 1910. It was originally founded by order of Queen Elizabeth I in 1563 as a grammar school.

Most of the school registers and log books are still with the schools or have been deposited with the Island Archives. The Ladies' College started in 1872. The Girls' Grammar School was founded in 1895 and a history was published in 1995 to celebrate their centenary. In 1985 it amalgamated with the Boys' Intermediate to form the Guernsey Grammar School.

There are several Roman Catholic schools in the island, including St Mary and St Michael, Blanchelande and Notre Dame. During the Second World War many of the pupils in Guernsey schools were evacuated to England and a recent book, *Torteval School in Exile*, describes the difficulties that the headmaster had in maintaining a school in Alderley Edge, near Manchester. Les Vauxbelets College was run by the De La Salle Brothers and was evacuated to Altrincham; after the war, the Brothers returned to Guernsey, and the College in Altrincham became St Ambrose College, now run by the Irish Christian Brothers. Blanchelande College moved to Les Vauxbelets in 1999.

Employment

As in all the Channel Islands, the inhabitants lived from farming and fishing, but there was a difference of degree in how they lived. In the *Saturday Magazine* for 21 March 1840, an article on Guernsey and Sark describes the lives of the ordinary people in more detail:

of the country people generally, we may say that they belong to three different classes, – the substantial land-owner, the small proprietor, and the cottager. The first class live upon the least marketable part of their produce; feed their cattle on the parsnips and beet-root grown on their own grounds; make their spirits from their own potatoes, and cider from their own apples; with their other produce, they purchase lands or leases, and thus gradually increase their property. The second class pursues nearly the same course, but on a smaller scale. He has his one cow and a few pigs, and by being generally economical, is enabled to lay by a little store. Many of them too are carpenters, or masons, and earn an addition to their income by going out to work, their families not requiring all their attention. Some, who live near the coast, join the trade of fisherman to that of farmer. Three or four of them will club together in the purchase and keep the boat; they go out to fish, return with a load, and the wives carry the fish to market, while the husbands proceed to cultivate their grounds. The third class, the cottagers, are generally day-labourers, or form part of the family of a small proprietor. Even this class of persons contrive to save money. A very favourable character for morality is given to the humbler classes of the inhabitants of Guernsey.

At the end of the fifteenth century knitting became an essential part of the economy; wool was shipped from the staple port of Southampton and Guernsey stockings were said to have been owned by Queen Elizabeth and Mary, Queen of Scots. Many items were exported and merchants, such as the Priaulx family, dealt with the orders, which had to follow the latest fashion requirements as to pattern and colour. The Guernsey, as a sweater, seems to have evolved in the late eighteenth century and the island supplied the British Army with Guernseys for the garrison in Nova Scotia for winter warmth.

Although Guernsey sailors took part in the cod fishing off the Newfoundland Banks, it was never to the same extent as the Jerseymen. However, a new book by Gregory Stevens Cox, *The Guernsey Merchants and their World*, gives detailed information, including family details, on the merchants of St Peter Port in the Georgian era. They were particularly involved in the wine trade, making St Peter Port an entrepôt for English wine merchants. There is a very useful CD *Guernsey sailing Ships 1786–1935*, by John W. Sarre, produced by the Guernsey Museum. Crew lists for Guernsey ships are available on: http://history.foote-family.com/maritime/index.php. The Priaulx Library also has a list of Guernsey sailors at the Battle of Trafalgar.

Guernsey was particularly successful in its privateering enterprises and smuggling, and was hit badly when both effectively finished in the early nineteenth century. Both *The Maritime History of the Channel Islands* and *From Sail to Steam* by Caroline Williams give a great deal of information on the involvement of Guernsey in shipbuilding and trade. For more information on shipbuilding see: www.museums.gov.gg/ under Guernsey History 1800–1899.

Guernsey developed links with the fruit trade, especially in South America. Such was the importance of William Le Lacheur to Costa Rica that his ships feature on their stamps and coins; for much information see the history timeline for 1843 on the Guernsey Museum website: www.museums.gov.gg/. The island also built up a large and successful horticultural business growing grapes and tomatoes – see the history timeline for 1860 on the museum website. The main glasshouses in the island were also used for flowers, although they have in recent times become less productive due to high fuel costs. The National Trust for Guernsey has good displays on the tomato industry and on many other occupations.

An occupation that does not have much coverage is that of butchers, but Stephen Foote has done a great deal of interesting research on the background and families of the butchers in Guernsey – for further information see: http://history.foote-family.com/butchers/index.php.

It is clear that quarrying of granite has always played an important role in the history of the island from the earliest times. At first pebbles were exported, but in the nineteenth century the demand for paving in cities, particularly London, made this a major industry in Guernsey. Brickmaking was probably started in the late nineteenth century when there was a demand for fashionable houses in the New Town part of St Peter Port. There are still some brick chimneys remaining, which have recently been restored.

Tourism has been a large employer in Guernsey; hotel and restaurant workers have come from Portugal and, more recently, from Poland. The industry was probably at its height in the 1960s and 1970s, before cheaper 'package' holidays came along.

The Island Police Force started in the mid-nineteenth century and there is

A disused brick chimney, Oatlands, St Sampson, Guernsey, built in 1892

a history of the force and details of the police during the German Occupation available on: www.guernsey.police.uk/ccm/navigation/publications/. The Priaulx Library has lists in the almanacs and in other sources of the officials in Guernsey over the centuries, but for the clergy there is also a database that gives interesting information on their careers: www.theclergydatabase.org.uk/index.html.

Like Jersey, Guernsey has always taken advantage of its tax position and some unusual businesses have resulted. For example, in 1857, James Keiller & Son of Dundee, the celebrated pioneers of marmalade manufacture, set up a branch in Guernsey. Its purpose was to evade costly sugar duties, and in time it evolved into a base for the firm's nascent export trade. After 1874, when Britain permitted the free importing of sugar, the establishment lost much of its rationale, and it was closed down in 1879. Tobacco processing was another enterprise that started in the eighteenth century, making the most of the island's tax advantages.

Freemasonry was established in the islands from an early date and 10 May 1753 witnessed the birth of the first lodge in Guernsey: the Lily Tavern in St Peter Port. Later in the year, on 22 December, saw the appointment of Thomas Dobrée as the first Provincial Grand Master of 'the several Islands of Guernsey, Jersey, Alderney, Sark and Arme [now known as Herm] in the English Channel'. The German Authorities banned Freemasonry in the Islands and both the Masonic temples in Guernsey and the Masonic temple in Alderney were sacked and pillaged by the German forces.

After the Reformation the poor were taken care of by the Church and the parish and there are some records in the Island Archives. A small hostel with

Milk-can making in Guernsey, C.A. Martin & Sons Ltd, c.1950s

The former poor house at Les Islets, St Pierre du Bois, Guernsey, founded c.1750

room for travellers was set up by Thomas Le Marchant and his wife in St Peter Port about 1513; the chapel was dedicated to St Julian and by the early 1600s it had become a hospital for the poor and destitute of St Peter Port. The parish of St Pierre du Bois had an almshouse at Les Islets, donated to the parish by Thomas de Lisle.

By the early 1700s there were so many stranger poor, as well as locals, that a larger premises were needed. The Town Hospital was opened in 1743 for the poor of St Peter Port and those of the British garrison who were in need. In 1755 seven of the country parishes got together and opened the country hospital in the parish of Castel; St Pierre du Bois and Forest joined this later on.

The journals of the Town Hospital, which are indexed up to 1856, are kept in the Island Archives and are a rewarding resource, with a great deal of information. For further information see: http://user.itl.net/~glen/townhosp.html.

To give an example, the 'career' of one Samson Toy can be followed through the journals – 30 June 1838: 'Samson Toy born in the Parish [of St Peter Port], son of an Englishman, a drunk, aged about 50 was admitted to the Hospital after being recommended by the Douzaine.' 14 November 1839: 'Samson Toy – ivroque et fainéant [lazy and a drunkard] was arrested by the police and sent to the House of Separation.' Out he went and then came back again! 15 June 1840: 'readmitted after living a life of debauchery'. On 11 September 1840 Samson Toy and William Bell were sent to Plymouth to serve in the Royal Navy. They got drunk at the first opportunity, sneaked aboard the man o'war *San Joseph* and slept there overnight. Both were arrested and sent back to Guernsey unwanted on the 18th! On 26 October 1842 he was sent to the 'house of separation' for three months for breaking out and going on the run for fifteen days and given remission on 30 January 1843. He was freed on 9 December 1843 – sixteen days later, on the 25th, he was 'found in need and brought in, just in time for his Christmas dinner'. Samson was freed again on 22 July 1844, but ended up back in the house of separation by 8 August. By 1846 Samson's daughter had been picked up 'off the streets', unable to make a living any other way than prostitution. On 10 September Elizabeth Toy, aged 22, the daughter of Sampson Toy, described as a *prostituée*, was admitted suffering from *la maladie vinerienne*.

Many of the poor emigrated to Canada, the UK and Australia, if their fares could be paid by the trustees of the hospital. Sampson and Elizabeth both took advantage of the scheme. He left Guernsey on 21 April 1845 to go to the Gaspé; on 27 August 1847, Elizabeth boarded a ship with five other girls to Demerara in British Guiana, South America. The latter destination may seem unusual; however, the master of the Town Hospital had a brother-in-law who was a merchant there. How father and daughter fared is not recorded.

Many Guernsey children were apprenticed to masters in Jersey and vice versa; this tradition continues, with children usually being adopted in the island that is not that of their birth.

Crime

Criminal records (*livres en crime*) are in the Greffe in the Royal Court and date from 1563. As with other records in the Greffe, it is best to enquire about access to them through the Island Archives; they are in French and are not indexed. The Constables had the right of arrest until 1920 and they recorded what they did.

Castle Cornet was originally used as prison and, with a sense of the ironic, there is said to be an old Guernsey saying: *avoir une vue du château* (having a view of the castle), which meant that one was being sent to jail. A new prison was built in 1811, but was condemned by Elizabeth Fry during her visit in 1833; the prison was situated just behind the Royal Court in Lefebvre Street, St Peter Port, but moved to St Sampson in 1989.

Chapter 14

MILITARY AND MIGRATION

The Militia, Garrisons, Guernsey Soldiers and Sailors

Like Jersey, the militia in Guernsey was in existence from an early date, probably by at least the thirteenth century. Guernseymen did not have to serve outside the island, but were primarily used for self-defence. The Crown might call upon them to help if the king needed rescuing or if the mainland (i.e. England) fell into foreign hands. Information on those who served in the militia can be found in the almanacs, and there is a display at Castle Cornet on the Royal Guernsey Militia.

Guernseymen served in the British Army and the Navy: Admiral James Saumarez (1757–1836), who was second-in-command at the Battle of the Nile, commanded at the Battle of Algeciras and became 1st Baron de Saumarez. Major General Sir Isaac Brock (1769–1812) became a major figure in the history of Canada as administrator of Upper Canada; he was killed in the war of 1812.

Although Guernseymen served in the First World War, and two companies were formed by 1914, it was not until 1916 (when conscription came in) that the militia was put into abeyance and the Royal Guernsey Light Infantry (RGLI) was formed. In the Battle of Cambrai in November 1917, for example, the RGLI took an active part and suffered accordingly, with nearly 40 per cent casualties: one officer and fourteen soldiers were killed, eight officers and 266 men wounded, with a further 216 missing in action. In all 327 men died during the war – such high casualties had a devastating effect on the island. *Dieux Aix: God Help Us – The Guernseymen Who Marched Away 1914–1918* by Major Edwin Parks gives a full history with lists of all the men who served and what happened to them. The museum at Castle Cornet now has a full display on the RGLI. There are also printed rolls of honour and war memorials in the island. These should include Frenchmen from the island who joined the French armed forces.

The Channel Islands Great War Group has done considerable research and actively seeks further information and additional members. For further information on the Great War in the Channel Islands see: www.greatwarci.net and www.lightinfantry.org.uk/regiments/gli/gli_index.htm.

The experiences of a Guernsey woman, Ada Le Poidevin, as a member of the Salvation Army during the First World War, can be found on: www.adaswar.net/memorials/ci-mems/ci-memorials-gu-list.htm.

During the Second World War, Guernseymen enlisted in the British forces, particularly the Hampshire Regiment. The records for these men and those who enlisted in the Royal Navy or the Royal Air Force are the same for those from England. The names of those who died and who are buried in graves cared for by the Commonwealth Graves Commission can be found on: www.cwgc.org. Normally Guernseymen were not subject to impressment, but it may have happened if they were in an English port.

The British Army provided a garrison in the island from an early date; although it was mainly in the eighteenth and nineteenth centuries that soldiers were billeted on local families – until the building of Fort George, above St Peter Port. The garrison cemetery is still there, although the fort has now been redeveloped into luxury houses.

Migration

Guernsey people travelled all around the world and many settled abroad. Although children were sent to France for schooling, there is not much evidence of them settling there. However, merchants often placed their relatives in countries with which they were trading; a member of the Brehaut family, for example, was sent to Exmouth in the seventeenth century. In the eighteenth century, Pierre Frederic Dobrée was sent from Guernsey to Nantes to improve his knowledge of commerce; marrying a merchant's daughter there, he became an important merchant in the French East India Company. His son, Thomas, was sent back to Guernsey to be educated, and continued to build up the family business, expanding into China, and made a fortune, which he spent on works of art. His son, also called Thomas, created a museum, the Musée Thomas Dobrée, in Nantes, which contains much of the family's collection.

There were schemes for sending poor people as apprentices to the American colonies from the end of the seventeenth century. Some people went involuntarily; there are incidents of Guernseymen being kidnapped off the beaches.

Canada and America continued to attract emigrants and many left Guernsey after 1815, following the demise of privateering and smuggling opportunities, although there was an advertisement back in 1806 for a planned migration to Prince Edward Island. Between 1817 and 1819 there were 1,310 emigrants to the United States and Canada: 792 of them went to Baltimore, 360 to Philadelphia and the rest to Quebec. In the nineteenth century Guernsey County, Ohio was settled by more than fifty Guernsey families from 1806 onwards; prominent among them was the Sarchet family. Marion Turk's books, *The Quiet Adventurers in North America* and *The Quiet Adventurers in Canada*, list many of these emigrants.

Some Guernsey people were attracted by the discovery of the gold fields or opportunities for farming in Australia between 1854 and 1856 – 257 people left the island for Australia. David Kreckeler's book, *Guernsey Emigrants to Australia 1828–1899*, gives details of many of the families and individuals who went there. Migrants left from ports such as Southampton, Liverpool and Plymouth. Migration to New Zealand was another alternative, and there is information on them held by the New Zealand Genealogical Society.

Around 17,000 Guernsey people were evacuated from the island in 1940 – many of them were sent to the north-west of England, particularly Bury and Stockport. Almost all the schools were evacuated. The Channel Islands Refugee Committee was founded and their magazines have a lot of family history material. In almost every place that Channel Islanders settled they formed societies. For further information on the Second World War evacuees see: *No Cause for Panic: Channel Island Refugees 1940–45* by Brian Ahier Read. In 1942 people of British origin were deported from Guernsey to Germany; the story of their internment is told in *Islanders Deported* by Roger E. Harris.

Guernsey has always had people taking refuge in the island. Early Huguenot refugees in the sixteenth century included many families who would go on to provide rectors, such as Fautrat and Brévint; after the revocation of the Edict of Nantes in 1685, there was a further wave of immigration. The names of those who came to the island are included in 'Huguenot Names from Island Sources' by Spencer Carey Curtis, published in the Transactions of La Société Guernesiaise for 1941. Information on those who came from France can be found on: www.francegenweb.org/ or for those who came from the Poitou region in western France see: http://huguenotsfrance.org/france/poitou/poitou.htm.

The Huguenot Society of Great Britain and Ireland also has a lot of records, including those from the London and Southampton churches, which is where Channel Islanders and Huguenot refugees particularly went (www.huguenotsociety.org.uk/).

During the eighteenth century, apart from the garrison there were also English and French settlers, particularly merchants and those who laboured in the cooperage industry making barrels for wine. There were also a number of Scottish merchants who settled in Guernsey.

French Royalist refugees, including priests, came to the island following the French Revolution, but many did not stay for long. Antoine Rosseti, for example, was a musician from Normandy who ran the assembly rooms in St Peter Port. In the mid-nineteenth century, there were further refugees, especially political and religious ones. Victor Hugo, who had first lived in Jersey, came to Guernsey in 1855 and stayed for fifteen years; as well as his writings, he was generous to the poor of St Peter Port.

New shipping networks meant that, following the agricultural depression after 1815, many people left the West Country and Dorset and settled in Guernsey. Rose-Marie Crossan's book, *Guernsey 1814–1914: Migration and Modernisation*, is an invaluable resource for the background to this migration and how Guernsey reacted to it. By 1821 St Peter Port had a larger population than many of its neighbouring towns, such as Weymouth, Dartmouth or Granville.

Guernsey is fortunate in having some interesting records for the nineteenth century immigrants. As well as the various censuses (see above) the stranger register dates from 1892 and lists non-locals who arrived in Guernsey; it has been indexed and is in the Island Archives. It includes the birthplace, occupation and details of the family (if any).

PART FOUR

Alderney

Chapter 15

GENERAL DESCRIPTION OF THE GEOGRAPHY, HISTORY AND ADMINISTRATION

Third largest of the Channel Islands, Alderney is the most northerly and the nearest to the Normandy coast, which is only eight miles away. The island is roughly three miles by five, with cliffs on the south and two large cultivated areas, of about five hundred acres in total, called La Grande Blaye and La Petite Blaye, which were divided into strips.

It has never been easy to get to the island as it is surrounded by rocks – in particular, the infamous 'Casquets', which has been the scene of many shipwrecks, is about eight miles to the north-west of the island. The Alderney

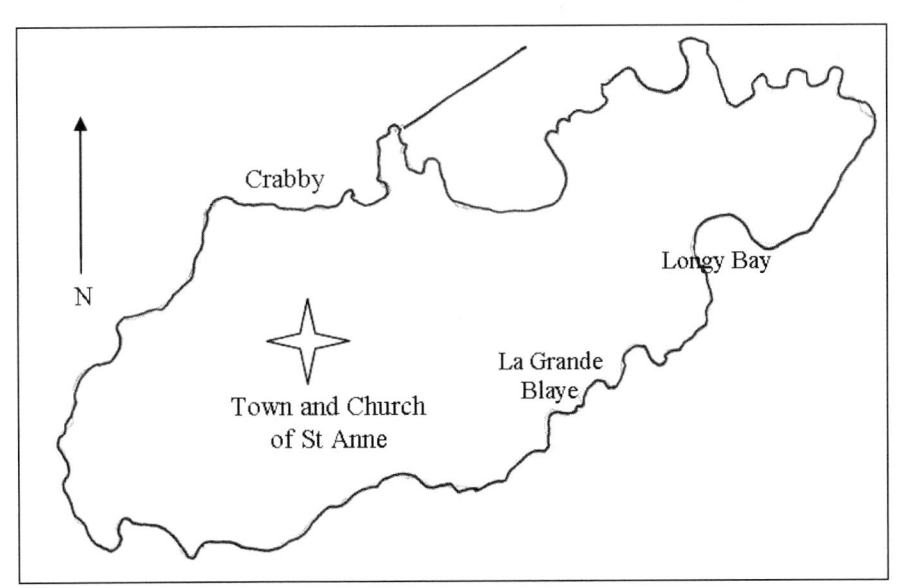

Map of the island of Alderney

The Marais, St Anne, Alderney, showing the watering place for the cattle that graze on La Grande and La Petite Blaye

Race (Le Raz), which is the passage between the island and France, has a tidal race of up to nine knots.

In the medieval period there were probably about 700 inhabitants. During the nineteenth century the population exploded with a large garrison and many workers building the forts and breakwater, so that there were nearly 5,000 inhabitants in 1861. Around 1,400 people lived in Alderney in 1940. In 2001 it had a population of about 2,294 and today there are about 2,400 inhabitants.

The town (*la ville*) of St Anne is situated in a small valley which runs to the north. Unlike the other Channel Islands, with a dispersed distribution of houses, nearly all the inhabitants lived in farmhouses, with barns and stables, in the town, although there are modern buildings now scattered around the island. The cattle were watered in Marais Square from a cattle trough as there was no water on La Grande or Petite Blaye. The Alderney cow was well known and the poet A.A. Milne referred to the Alderney cow in his poem *The King's Breakfast*.

The States of Alderney (the Legislature) consists of a President and ten States' members. In addition, two States of Alderney representatives are full members of the Guernsey States of Deliberation and take part in the government of the Bailiwick with full voting rights. Alderney has its own Royal Court with a chairman and six Jurats (judges of fact).

Like the other islands, Alderney is rich in megalithic remains and may have been a burial site for the inhabitants of what is now the French department of Manche in Normandy. The Romans may also have kept a garrison on the island. Known in French as Aurigny, the first documentary reference to Alderney is in 1042. Probably the earliest chapel was one dedicated to St Vignal (or Guenal) in the sixth century. There was a chapel dedicated to St Michel at Longis. In the tenth century the Bishop of Coutances owned the western half of the island and had a mill there; the eastern half was owned by the Duke of Normandy.

The parish church was originally granted to St Marie of Cherbourg and the settlement was named after her. However, by about 1654 the church became known as St Anne and the town was renamed accordingly. In the nineteenth century, when the population exploded with a garrison and construction workers, the church was deemed to be too small and only the clock tower and the cemetery remain. A new church designed by Sir George Gilbert Scott was built on a new site in 1850 and was also dedicated to St Anne.

At first the island was leased by the Chamberlin family and then in 1684 the Le Mesurier family became the hereditary governors. There is a painting of Jean Le Mesurier and his wife being granted the governorship of Alderney in the Island Hall; it depicts the couple with a map of the island.

The islanders were renowned for smuggling and privateering, and much of the wealth of the island came from these two activities, but they came to an end when smuggling was stopped in 1806 and privateering finished when Napoleon was defeated at Waterloo in 1815.

The island became heavily fortified particularly during the nineteenth century because of French threats, but also much earlier in the mid-sixteenth century and through the seventeenth and eighteenth centuries. The harbour at Braye was built from 1847 onwards specifically to keep an eye on the French at Cherbourg.

In 1847 when Queen Victoria and Prince Albert visited the island, she had

The Island Hall. Built in about 1660 by Nicholas Ling, Governor of Alderney, it was then rebuilt and enlarged in 1763 by the current governor at the time, Jean Le Mesurier, and became known as Government House.

time to do some paintings, including a charming one of an Alderney girl wearing a large white headdress that looks very French in origin. A British Army officer, Captain George Wood, had been stationed in Alderney in 1815 and wrote later of the charms of the local girls, several of whom had married his fellow officers.

In the late 1840s many families of Cornish, Irish, Dorset and French descent came to the island to help build the fortifications. The great breakwater was started in 1847, but was repeatedly destroyed and continues to be a source of financial concern for islanders, as it is now the responsibility of the Bailiwick of Guernsey as a contribution to the defence of the British Isles.

In 1940, once France fell to the Germans, given the choice between evacuating and remaining, almost the entire population elected to leave after a mass meeting at Les Butes. They were taken to Weymouth, England, on 23 June. Once the Germans arrived on 2 July, most of the handful of people that had stayed were moved to Guernsey, and Alderney was once again fortified. A few people, however, did remain on the island throughout the Occupation. Slave labour was used to build this stronghold, administered by the infamous Organisation Todt, and probably about 400 people died on the island.

Once the Occupation was over, the island had to be made safe again with a mine-clearance operation; sadly, a soldier of the Royal Engineers was killed during this operation. On 15 December (now a public holiday) 1945 the first party of islanders came home; the remainder followed gradually, when Alderney could once again support them.

Since then the island has become a holiday destination, though there are also several finance and Internet companies based there.

Chapter 16

CIVIL RECORDS AND CENSUSES

Although many of the official records were destroyed during the Occupation, luckily the civil registers were taken to Guernsey and consequently survived. The Greffier of the Royal Court (QEII Street, St Anne, Alderney GY9 3AA) is the registrar for births, marriages, deaths, companies and land. If you require a copy of a certificate, there is a charge of £17.50, which includes postage to any destination; there is no search fee.

All family history enquiries, however, are sent to the family history volunteer who has copies of all of the records, both civil and ecclesiastical. As all enquiries are sent to her, there is no need to write to several places for information. The present volunteer is Mrs Eileen Mignot, who took over from the late Mrs Peggy Wilson, who had built up a large collection; she is assisted by Alison Osborne. Mrs Mignot does not make a charge, but welcomes donations, which are used for rebinding the collection and are also donated to local charities.

The civil registers started on 25 July 1850 for births and 2 August 1850 for deaths, though marriages did not begin until 1924. There is a gap in the registration of births between May 1871 and December 1874. There is a hand-ruled book of declarations, from August 1850 to December 1874, that can be used to fill this gap. There is a similar gap from 1875 until 1907 for the deaths but there is also a hand-ruled book of declarations from October 1855 to December 1874.

Copies of the births, deaths and marriages from 1925 to date are kept at the Guernsey Greffe. The Priaulx Library, St Peter Port, Guernsey has incomplete microfilmed sets of civil registration records as follows: births, July 1850 until August 1885, and deaths, 1850–55 and 1907–25. There are marriages from 1886 (from St Anne's Church only) and from 1891 onwards from elsewhere on the island. There are no records of civil registration during the German Occupation from 1940 until December 1945.

There is no adoption register as adoptions are organised through Guernsey.

Censuses were taken with the rest of the Bailiwick of Guernsey. In 1821 the population was 1,154, by 1831 it had slightly decreased to 1,045 and stayed at that level in 1841 when it was 1,038. However, the population exploded in 1851 when it stood at 3,333, when the military fortifications started and by 1861 had reached 4,932. In 1871 the population had shrunk to 2,738. In 1881 it was 2,048; 1891, 1,857; 1901, 2,062; 1911, 2,561; 1921, 1,598; and 1931, 1,521. The censuses are available on the main family history sites and on microfilm at the Priaulx Library in Guernsey. The use of English was more widespread than in the other islands, nevertheless some Christian names may have been translated; for example, someone who is named Peter may have been christened Pierre.

Indexes to the inhabitants of Alderney in the censuses can be found in the Guernsey census indexes, copies of which are at the Priaulx Library, Guernsey (and at the Lord Coutanche Library, Jersey), but they are not separately indexed.

A page from the book of persons wishing to return to Alderney, from those who had left the island in 1940. By kind permission of the Alderney Society Museum.

Peter Hamer's website (http://sites.google.com/site/alderneylocal history/Home) includes transcriptions of the censuses for 1841, 1851, 1861, 1871, 1881, 1891 and 1901. Lorna Pratt's website of the 1841 census for the Channel Islands (http://members.shaw.ca/jerseymaid/alderney.html) includes Alderney, but the transcription is not complete. There is a census of Alderney property and inhabitants as it was in June 1940; this is kept in the Alderney Society Museum.

There is a handwritten card index to the names of all the people who were evacuated. It is possible that at least one family stayed, although it is suggested that up to seven farmers remained on the island throughout the Occupation. The form was sent to Alderney families in 1942, two years after the evacuation, and not all were returned, so there are some gaps. The completed forms give a great deal of information, both about the individuals and their immediate families and other relations – births of children and deaths, and details of occupations, maiden names of wives and widows and the properties lived in, plus the contents of their houses when the hurried evacuation commenced.

Chapter 17

CHURCH REGISTERS, NAMES AND CEMETERIES

The baptism registers for the parish of St Anne start in 1662, the marriages from 1657 and the burials from 1652. Before the German Occupation the registers were taken to Winchester, although the most recent book was left in Guernsey. The books were returned to the island sometime after the liberation.

There are, however, gaps in the registers, as sometimes there was no resident rector in Alderney and each of the Guernsey ministers would pay a visit in turn; this was not regarded as a very popular duty. The Reverend Thomas Picot (1658–1721), writing in about 1700, (see: *Three Seventeenth-Century Clergymen* by M.R. Bielby in the CIFHS journal summer 1979, winter 1979 and spring 1980) complained that the Dean (of Guernsey, Alderney and Sark) had been giving licences for marriages without banns and taking the money, which left the minister who performed the service out of pocket. Thomas stated that he would perform marriages without fees, without delay and even for strangers.

Copies of certificates for baptisms and marriages can be obtained from the rector, the Reverend Stephen Masters at the New Vicarage, St Anne, Alderney GY9 3XA (phone: 01481 824866). The family history volunteer, Mrs Eileen Mignot, has copies of the Church of England registers and enquiries should be addressed to her. Mrs Mignot, most usefully, has copies of everything to do with family history in Alderney, whether it is the civil registers, the Church of England registers, the non-conformist registers or the census. She also has about 200 family trees, including information on families who came to build the breakwater. In the collection there are correspondence files, cuttings, obituaries and photos. There is also a scrapbook with information on all the churches and chapels, past and present.

There are copies in the Priaulx Library (St Peter Port, Guernsey) of the Alderney Church of England registers 1780–1832 for baptisms, 1819–27 for private baptisms, marriages 1841–86 and burials 1809–12 and 1853–9.

There is a splendid description in a letter of a wedding that took place in Alderney on 7 September 1779 (published in the Transactions of La Société Guernesiaise, 1926). The letter was written by 17-year-old Marthe Le Mesurier, sister of the groom, Pierre Le Mesurier (later to become the

St Anne's Church, Alderney. It was built between 1847 and 1850 and designed by Sir George Gilbert Scott, to cater for the large garrison. It was paid for by the Reverend Canon John Le Mesurier in memory of his parents.

penultimate hereditary governor) who married his cousin, Marie Le Mesurier:

> Two large Tents were erected upon the two Grass Plots that are before our House . . . A large ox was killed. Three dozen of Chickens were led to Execution and two dozen of Pidgeons received sentence of Death. Five tongues and eight large Hams mounted Guard, and Wine was like Silver in the Days of Solomon. . . . The Rich Cake not being come from London we had some made in our house. Seven large seed Cakes and seven plum cakes, in all 180 pounds, were made at home. 1,000 biscuits were had from Guernsey . . . At last Tuesday morning appeared and found us in glee and hurry. Our newly landed Folks were all stripped of their sables and dressed by us in Colours. Peter had on a white coat, and breeches trimmed with spangled lace and green ribband, with the lining of the same colour as the ribband, of a very delicate sea-green, and a silver tissue waistcoat with small flowers over it. Mary, from top to toe was in immaculate white and looked better than ever I had seen her. . . . Before four o'clock in the afternoon most of the company were assembled. A little after four, six

young boys and six girls were called out, and green branches being put in their hands they preceded the Bride who walked between my Father and Nicholas Le Mesurier [the bride's brother]. Then the bridegroom and his two supporters, Miss Betsey Dobrée and Miss Anley. Then we all followed, two by two, between a vast crowd of people that filled the Church, fuller than it has ever been since the dedication of it. The noise and bustle that ensued flurried little Mary, and during the Ceremony she shook a great deal, but throughout the whole affair she behaved exceedingly well. . . . Master Peter has a bold face of his own and the Courage of the Le Mesuriers never forsook him. After the ceremony all the Cockades [invitees] repaired to our House, while the rest of the people went to the Mouriaux [another house] and the publick houses, where Burnt Wine and Biscuits were given to those who would have it. When we came home we all ranged ourselves under the tents to drink Burnt Wine and eat Biscuits by way of whetting our Spirits a little. Immediately after we had tea in the same place, and, considering the vast concourse of people that assembled, were served exceedingly well, one servant stationed to one Tea-pot. After that the Nobility retired to the Great, and the Gentry in the little, Parlour. In the latter place one Fiddler attended for Jiggs and in the other another played Minuets, together with a boy that plays upon the pipe. . . . These Minuets continued till Eight o'clock, when everybody were called out to see the fireworks. . . . The surprize [sic] of our folks beggars description. They were frightened at first, but grew soon familiar to the Stars and the Suns, whom they almost worship'd. But the last grand Piece had the best effect. It was a laurel tree in the shape of a Pyramid. Two joint hearts appeared in the middle, with 'P' on one side and 'M' on the other, and 'L.M.' was fixed over the hearts. . . . While we had been at the fireworks supper had been put under the Tents and most people fell to it upon their return. When we had all sup'd and began dancing contre-danses and jigs the door was locked . . . (until) six o'clock the next morning, when not a soul had strength enough to make up another dance. Mary went to bed at ten, but slip'd upstairs unperceived by any but me . . . Mrs Goslin and Mrs Nicholas Le Mesurier that went upstairs by chance at the same time put her in bed. An hour after, Havilland [the bridegroom's brother] led all the Company to the Bride's door and gave three thundering Huzza's, and that ceremony was twice again repeated in the course of the night.

John Wesley visited Alderney in 1787 and preached near the harbour. A Methodist chapel was built in 1790 off Victoria Street by wealthy people in Alderney (although it seems likely that people were probably still married in the Church of England); it was replaced in 1814 with one in Church Street and a larger one was built at Les Butes in 1852. Originally, the circuit was

Alderney Methodist Chapel, Les Butes, built in 1852

French-speaking, but with the arrival of the garrison and workers, an English-speaking circuit was established.

A Presbyterian chapel was built later (c.1850) in St Anne. The Primitive Methodists had a church in the High Street which was in use 1840–70 and is now the Salvation Army citadel. The Methodist, Presbyterian and Primitive records were almost all lost during the Occupation, although a few records are extant; however, a copy of the non-Anglican marriage book, covering 1892–1930, was copied by Mrs Wilson from the Greffe.

The Catholics (post-Reformation) re-established themselves in 1812 and built a chapel at Crabbé in 1848 and there are records for baptisms 1849–1952, marriages 1852–1924 and burials 1858–1940 (Note that some of the records are in Latin). That chapel was destroyed during the German Occupation. Since 1958 the new Catholic Church, St Anne and St Mary Magdelene, is off the Braye Road in St Anne. The Priaulx Library in Guernsey has copies of the Roman Catholic register baptisms for 1858–61 and 1874.

Surnames and Christian Names

In the 1309 assize rolls for the Channel Islands, the names of Duplain, Hougez, Le Vallée and Pezet are mentioned and these are names that still exist in the island today. Immigrants from Guernsey, probably in the fifteenth century, included those with the surnames of Ollivier, Flerre and Le Cocq. The two waves of Huguenot refugees saw the arrival of several families such as the Hérivels (later to emigrate to Jersey and then Australia), and Gaudions, probably from Normandy.

Not all those who came from France were Huguenot refugees: the Mignot family came from Cap de la Hague in about 1654, and the Jean family probably came about the same time. The family of Gauvain may have come from Brittany. In the nineteenth century numerous families settled in the island and some stayed; there were also the garrisons and the men who came to build the breakwater and the fortifications.

People from Alderney who were born, married and died outside the island are known as strays and their records have been published in La Société Guernesiaise Family History Journal.

Cemeteries

The cemetery of the old demolished Church of England church of St Marie is still in existence with several gravestones, near to the Alderney Museum in the town of St Anne. The new Church of England church of St Anne has a large graveyard all around it.

La Cimitière de St Michel is on the Longis Road. This was the strangers' cemetery from 1806 and has a new section. The Roman Catholic cemetery is also here. Until 1961 there was a German cemetery adjacent, but the bodies were exhumed and taken to Normandy.

There is no crematorium on the island, so anyone wishing their body to be cremated has to be taken to Guernsey and the records are consequently kept there.

The war memorial for the two world wars is in Victoria Street and a list of the names can be found on: http://user.itl.net/~glen/alderneywar.html and also on www.greatwarci.net.

Chapter 18

PROPERTY AND OFFICIAL RECORDS

It is likely that the Royal Court of Alderney would originally have met out of doors at Le Huret, but in 1770 a courthouse was built, which still stands in QEII Street, although it had to be rebuilt after the Occupation. This is also used for meetings of the States.

Sadly, during the German Occupation of 1940–45 all the following records were destroyed: the Land Registry, the Royal Court records and the minutes of the States of Alderney. There is a project now underway to find all Alderney documents not in the island, particularly those in Guernsey. Some of these can be found in the Island Archives, St Peter Port, Guernsey.

Since 1949 the Land Registry records the title of properties and these are tied to a map; all these records are kept in the Royal Court of Alderney. The cadastre in St Peter Port also keeps records. To compensate for the loss of the Land Registry records Alderney is fortunate to have a map of 1831 showing the ownership of the common lands.

In 1825 the Le Mesurier family, who had been governors of Alderney for several generations, surrendered their patent to the Crown and left the island for richer pastures. They left because Alderney was not prospering. Smuggling had been all but stamped out in 1808, and the end of the Napoleonic wars in 1815 dispensed with the need for a British garrison and so privateering ended. The islanders had quickly become poverty stricken once these sources of revenue had been removed and many were forced from the sea (and other trades) back to the land.

However, the growth of the population to around 1,000 during more prosperous times meant that the open-field system at La Blaye was no longer enough to feed everyone. It was soon realised that more agricultural land would be needed to help the island's fifty-two families fend for themselves. The Guernsey orders in council of the period record that:

> on the 11th day of June in the year 1823 the inhabitants assembled in the temple at the tolling of the bells at 9 o'clock in the morning in consequence of a Publication made from the Pulpit the preceding Sunday in the customed manner to take into consideration the report of the committee composed of nine persons chosen the 27th of May 1823,

from the respectable inhabitants, for the purpose of forming a plan which would be most advantageous for dividing the common lands. [The land] should be divided equally among the inhabitants great or small without distinction of sex or age.

The vote decided that the division should consist of 104 portions, 52 of good land and 52 of inferior. The long-standing families were divided up into fifty groups, each nominated one person to draw lots for the good land and inferior land. The four lots left over were to be left for a period of time to allow for late claimants who may have been off the island when the process began.

The plans finally came before the King, William IV, at the Court of St James on 4 August 1830 and were refined as follows: the division was agreed and the four remaining lots were to be held for eight months to allow for the 1831 census to be taken and 'to give time for those who may have been omitted to come forward'. Leftovers were to be at the disposal of the Crown. Someone was to be named as surveyor and 'a book should be kept to be deposited in the Greffe Office to be referred to in future.'

Parts to be put aside before the division took place included 100 feet from the highwater mark in the north-west from the Clonque to the Manneze for the use of the militia or any future British garrison and another area nearby for drying *vraic*. An area for quarrying was also to be reserved on the south side of the island. It was ordered that a copy of the order 'be affixed to the

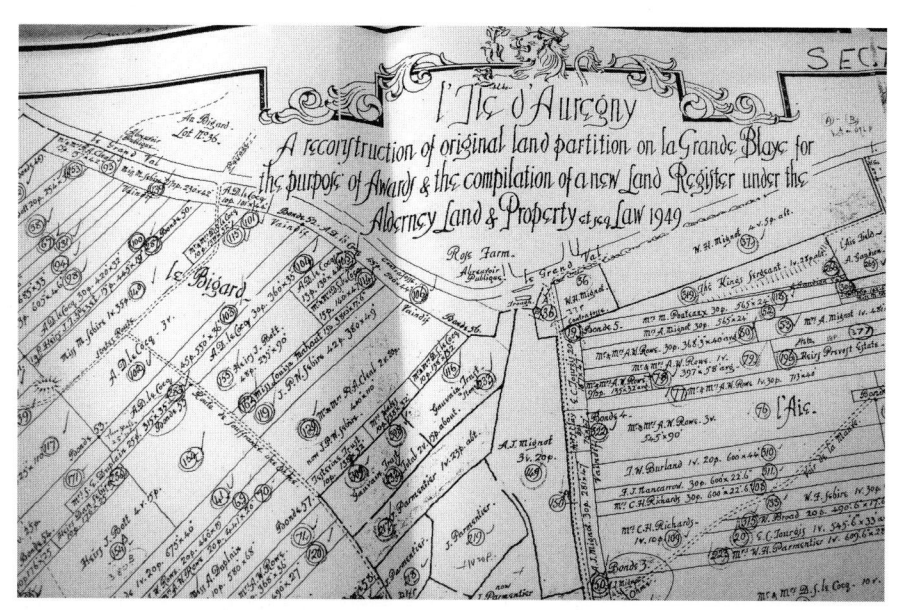

Part of the map of Alderney in 1949, showing the distribution of land in the island. By kind permission of the Alderney Society Museum.

church door for four successive Sundays from completion'. The Royal Court of Guernsey was warned to 'allow the names of those born during this period to be added and those who have died to be expunged' with the costs of applications to be borne by the islanders. A book was indeed made, complete with a full listing of all the families who earned the right to the land and detailed maps of each area. Copies survive in both Alderney (at the Alderney Society Museum, High Street, Alderney GY9 3TG) and in Guernsey in the Greffe. It is entitled *Plans des Communes de l'Ile d'Auregny* (Plan of the Commons of the Island of Alderney).

Each of the large pages contains a list of named and numbered lots, and nineteen people in all are included per lot. The head of household is at the top of the list, wives and families below. Widowed heads of household are indicated. A corresponding map appears opposite with each lot indicated. Areas used for other purposes, for instance the cemetery and the *Enclos du Ministre* and land reserved for the Government (including the pre-breakwater Braye harbour) are indicated.

Another useful map is that of 1949, a copy of which is in the Alderney Museum. This shows all the landowners as of that date. A survey of the buildings of Alderney was compiled by Charles Brett and this gives historical, as well as architectural, information.

Wills of realty since 1949 are registered by the Royal Court of Alderney and copies can be ordered from them. Wills of personalty are with the Ecclesiastical Court of Guernsey.

Chapter 19

EDUCATION, EMPLOYMENT AND CRIME

Education

Earlier rectors (when there was one in the island) may have instructed children – particularly boys – and around 1700 the *Douzaine* was ordered by the Canon Laws to set up a parish school. The *Douzeniers* complained that they could not afford the fees for a schoolmaster and that although the rector could teach children their catechism, he did not have time to teach them to read and write.

Old church tower of St Marie's, Alderney, with the old boys' school on the left, which is now the Alderney Museum.

The Alderney Society Museum is situated in the old school, built in 1792 by the Governor, John Le Mesurier, which was for boys only; girls went to a private school established in the house of Mrs Le Mesurier, Les Mouriaux, in 1817.

In 1851 the parish church schools were under Henry H. Langstaff, of St John's College, Battersea, who was the master. There was a Methodist church in Church Street 1861–71. There were also two dame schools: one ran by the Misses Le Lièvre in the High Street and the other by Mrs Todd out at Le Braye. Today there is a school, St Anne's, for 4–16-year-olds and a private primary school called Ormer House.

Employment

The Alderney commercial directory of 1851 gives a flavour of the kind of occupations in the island: there were, for example, six bakers and flour dealers, a billiards-room keeper, three glass, china and earthenware dealers, three ironmongers and two watchmakers. Not unexpectedly, there were nine publicans and four hotel and lodging-house keepers, three of whom were women. There were also three surgeons and four tailors.

Agriculture was important in the island, even though there were few fields and farmers probably fished as well. There has been some debate as to whether Jersey and Guernsey cattle were passed off as Alderneys in the hope of raising a higher price; or perhaps Alderneys were simply smaller Guernseys. It is possible that the Reverend Elie Picot bred the first Alderneys; the last pure-bred Alderney is believed to have been born in 1927.

It was not until 1802 that a Freemasons' lodge was formed in Alderney when the Olive Lodge No. 328 was warranted on 13 July of that year.

Crime

Originally there was a lock-up near the marketplace in St Anne, though traditionally prisoners were looked after by the *Prévôt*, who had to keep them locked up as best he could, sometimes just in a room on which he would keep guard. Criminal cases were referred to the Royal Court of Guernsey and records are, therefore, kept there. Some cases are reported in the Guernsey newspapers.

The prison was built in 1850 alongside the Royal Court House (built in 1772) in St Anne, but the records were destroyed during the German Occupation. The prison is still in use as a lock-up, but long-term prisoners serve their sentences in Guernsey.

Chapter 20

MILITARY AND MIGRATION

As in the other Channel Islands, Alderney had a militia composed of all men between the ages of 16 and 60. The militia would be less effective at some periods than others, probably when the threat was low; in 1793 when Peter Le Mesurier became Governor mention was made of a lack of uniform, weapons and discipline. In the late 1790s the Methodists refused to do drills on Sunday and eventually they formed their own company, which had to do extra drills during the rest of the week.

The Alderney Society has compiled a list of garrisons stationed in the island from 1732; this is displayed in the Alderney Museum. Some regiments would have served in the other Channel Islands. They include the 18th Royal Irish Regiment (1732–85), the 2nd/5th Northumberland Fusiliers (1806–7) and the 1st Battalion Seaforth Highlanders (1820–24).

From 1824 until 1852 there were no regular army units in Alderney; there was always a regimental depot (recruiting and training company) in Guernsey and they may have visited Alderney. The garrison revived again in 1852, when the 11th Field Company (RE) arrived and also when the forts were largely completed, by about 1861. During this period, it is interesting to note that from 1876 to 1877 the 104th Bengal Fusiliers (later 2nd Battalion Royal Munster Fusiliers) were garrisoned in Guernsey and Alderney.

During the Great War there were usually infantry on the island. These were generally 'garrison' battalions or the Royal Defence Corps, composed of low-medical-grade troops, in whom the parent regiment were not much interested. An exception was the 4th Battalion North Staffordshire Regiment that was in Alderney from August 1914 until September 1916: it was the officer training unit.

After the Great War the infantry garrison does not appear to have been taken very seriously. Although there was nominally a battalion in Guernsey and Alderney, it was often represented in Alderney by one platoon only, the rest being elsewhere – including strike duty in England and police duties in Ireland. The regiments and dates of first arrival were: November 1919, 2nd Battalion Royals (North Lancashire) Regiment; February 1922, 1st Battalion Manchester Regiment; October 1924, 2nd Battalion Duke of Cornwall's Light Infantry; November 1927, 2nd Battalion Queen's Own Royal West Kent Regiment; November 1936, 2nd Battalion Sherwood Foresters; November 1938, 1st Battalion Royal Irish Fusiliers.

The breakwater and harbour of Alderney, showing the arrival of the Courier *c.1905*

The Invalids' and later the Veterans' Battalions were separate regiments manned with volunteers who had been previously discharged from regular service on account of wounds, age or illness. Being of limited physical capability, the veterans had only a home-defence role or light duties (and thus were ideal for Channel Islands service). Muster returns for both Invalid Companies and Veterans' Battalions are in the War Office archives in The National Archives, in WO12. Casualty returns for the Veterans' Battalions 1809–30 are in WO25/2190–2195 and 2216–2243.

In the Alderney Society Museum there is an excellent catalogued photographic collection, particularly of ships, along with a great deal of material on the evacuation. There are separate catalogues to the documents, relating for example to the harbours, ships and buildings. There are also scrapbooks and press cuttings. The Alderney Society's website is: www.alderney society.org/society.html.

Migration

In the 1660s the States of Guernsey recommended that poor children from Alderney should be sent to the American colonies.

As mentioned in previous chapters, French migrants settled in the island from the earliest times. The British migrants came to work in the island, particularly in the nineteenth century, and many stayed on. Men and women also came from Guernsey; for example, Nicholas Lihou who was born in

1826 in St Peter Port came to Alderney before 1854 with his Guernsey-born wife, Adele, and was the superintendent of the harbour works in 1871 and foreman of the Admiralty works in the 1881 census.

Many Irish came to Alderney after the 1840s and the 1861 census shows that more than half of the inhabitants were not born in the Channel Islands. Many of those who came to Alderney in the nineteenth century then moved to Guernsey and later Jersey seeking work. The Bott family did precisely this and eventually some of the family then emigrated to Australia.

PART FIVE

Sark

Chapter 21

GENERAL DESCRIPTION OF THE GEOGRAPHY, HISTORY AND ADMINISTRATION

Sark is the fourth largest of the Channel Islands and the smallest of the substantially inhabited islands. It is situated six miles to the east of Guernsey, fourteen miles to the north-west of Jersey and is twenty-four miles from the French coast. About three miles in length and a mile and a half wide, the larger part of the island is sometimes known as Great Sark, whilst Little Sark, a small peninsula to the south, is connected by a narrow bridge high above the cliffs, known as La Coupée. It was a treacherous route in high winds and children going to school would have to crawl across; now it has railings along its length. The island is surrounded by high cliffs, about

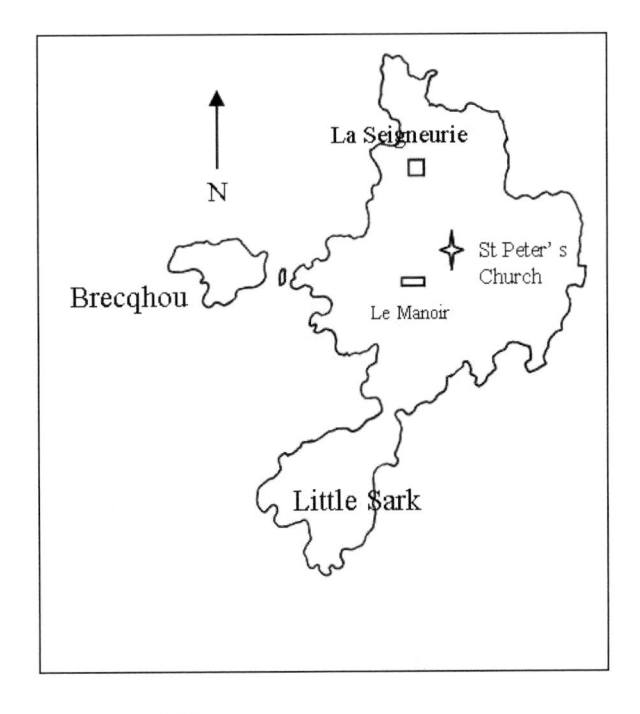

Map of Sark and Brecqhou

300 feet high, with few landing places, although there are two small harbours adjacent to each other on the east coast.

A small island to the west of Sark is Brecqhou, also known as L'Isle aux Marchands, after the Le Marchand family who claimed it in the seventeenth century. It was used for hunting rabbits and seasonal grazing, but it appears that no house was built on it until 1836. The *Seigneur* of Sark leased it to various farmers from between 1797 and 1929, when Mrs Hathaway, the Dame of Sark, sold it as a tenement to Angelo Clarke. In 1993 Brecquou was bought by twin brothers Sir Frederick and Sir David Barclay,who subsequently built a castle and developed a small community there.

Although Sark was settled from Jersey, the shorter distance from Guernsey has gradually had more influence over its laws, trade and communications. Sark, including Brecqhou, is part of the Bailiwick of Guernsey, but has its own government, the Chief Pleas (*Chiefs Plaids*), and criminal court. Its Court of Appeal is the Royal Court of Guernsey. Sark's power to legislate for itself dates from 1583. Chief Pleas originally consisted of the *Seigneur* and his forty tenants, with a Greffier and *Prévôt*. From 1675 Sark's Judge and four *Jurés* were replaced by a *Seneschal*. There were no elections until 1922, when twelve People's Deputies were added. Under the new

The old windmill, Sark. Built in 1571 by order of the Seigneur, Helier de Carteret, *it stands 375 feet above sea level. A working model is now on show in the Sark Museum.*

constitution of 2008, apart from the *Seigneur* and *Seneschal* as president, all twenty-eight members, *Conseillers*, are elected by universal suffrage. The *Seneschal* was both the Judge and the presiding officer of the Chief Pleas, but the two roles have now been separated.

There is a Constable and a *Vingtenier* who are responsible for policing.

By the early nineteenth century there were about 400 inhabitants. In 1841 the population increased sharply to 790 as the result of a silver-mining boom after 1835 that had collapsed, however, by 1847. There is a permanent population of about 600 today.

Sark was inhabited from Neolithic times, and had an early Christian settlement of up to sixty-two monks with a population in the thirteenth century of about 300. After the Black Death in 1349, and following continuous French raids, the island was almost deserted; by about 1500 only pirates seem to have lived there. Following a French military occupation from 1549 to 1552 the English Crown became concerned about Sark's vulnerability and the possibility of it being used to launch an attack on the other Channel Islands.

In 1563 Helier de Carteret, son of the *Seigneur* of St Ouen in Jersey, farmed Sark for two years and in 1565 he obtained a land grant from Queen

Le Manoir, Sark. This was the home of Helier de Carteret of St Ouen, Jersey, Seigneur of Sark, who resettled the island in 1565. To the right is a long building that was used as the temple and as a school house.

Elizabeth I. The terms of his Letters Patent obliged him to inhabit Sark with at least forty men, with arms for defence. He formed the original *quarantaine* (forty) by granting out lands in perpetual lease to his chosen followers: Calvinists seeking religious freedom. To put a stop to tenants dividing their lands among their heirs (and endangering a family livelihood) division of tenements was forbidden by King James I in 1611. Confiscation of the fief in 1643 and exile of the Royalist *Seigneur* during the English Civil War led to some dismemberment of tenements, not all of which were reassembled after the restoration of the king. The last de Carteret *seigneurs* created further properties by selling off parcels of original manorial lands.

By about 1600 Sark's Chief Pleas of 'inhabitants' consisted only of the forty tenants and remained so until 1922.

During the seventeenth century the Le Gros family from Guernsey, acquired a lot of property in Sark – so much so that Suzanne Le Pelley, daughter of Judge Jean Le Gros, was able to purchase the fief and became the Dame. Prior to 1730, the *Seigneurie* was at Le Manoir, the house of the first *Seigneur*, Helier de Carteret. Suzanne Le Pelley retained the family tenement of La Perronerie, which was built on the site of the sixth-century monastery founded by St Magloire, and it became the *Seigneurie*. In 1852 Dame Marie Collings, daughter of a Guernsey privateer called Jean Allaire, purchased the fief and her son, the Reverend William T. Collings, enlarged the house and improved the grounds. He also gave the church its chancel. The current *Seigneur*, Michael Beaumont, inherited the island from his grandmother, Dame Sybil Hathaway, on her death in 1974; she was the granddaughter of Reverend Collings.

There are no cars in Sark, although tractors are used, but most people walk or use a bicycle. Horse-drawn carriages are also popular. Travel to Sark is only possible by boat from Guernsey or Jersey.

Chapter 22

CIVIL RECORDS AND CENSUSES

The civil registration of births, marriages and deaths started in Sark in 1925 and copies are obtainable from the Greffe, La Chasse Marette, Sark GY9 0SF; telephone 01481 832012. If visiting the island, then the Greffier's office hours are 2.30 p.m.–4 p.m., Tuesday, Wednesday and Friday.

Copies are kept at the Guernsey Greffe (see Directory) and are available from there. They cost £17.50 each, but they are also available from the Priaulx Library: microfilmed copies are £1 per entry. Most births now take place in Guernsey, but occasionally a mother does not make it or the weather is too inclement. Marriages take place at St Peter's Anglican Church and the Methodist Church, and civil marriages take place at the Sark Greffe. Cremations take place in Guernsey.

As in the other islands the census for Sark has been taken since 1821, although The National Archives confirm that the copies of the household schedules for 1861 are missing. The population in 1821 was 488, in 1831 was 543, but in 1841 was 785, due to the opening of the silver mines and the Cornish mine workers who came to work in them. In 1851 the numbers had returned to previous levels at 580 people. There was little change from then on: in 1861 the population was 583; by 1871, 546; 1881, 578; 1891, 570; 1901, 506; and in 1911, 579. In 1921 it rose slightly to 611 but decreased in 1931 to 571.

There were five people living on Brecqhou in 1845, and although deserted at times, the permanent population has never increased greatly until the 1990s, when several families lived there.

The censuses have been indexed by volunteers of the Family History Section of La Société Guernesiaise for 1841, 1851, 1871, 1881 and 1901 and are bound together with the volumes for Guernsey, which are available at the Priaulx Library, St Peter Port, Guernsey or the Lord Coutanche Library, St Helier, Jersey. Note that the 1861 census is missing.

On Lorna Pratt's website (http://members.shaw.ca/jerseymaid/Serketc.html) there is a transcription of the 1841 census.

The 1911 census is (at the time of writing) available only on: www.1911census.co.uk (a subscription service owned by Find My Past), but should be available freely from 2012.

Chapter 23

CHURCH REGISTERS, NAMES AND CEMETERIES

The islands of Sark and Brecqhou today consist of one Church of England parish, that of St Peter.

The first chapel in Sark was that of St Magloire which was situated where La Seigneurie (La Perronerie) now is. When Helier de Carteret received the Letters Patent from Queen Elizabeth I in 1588, part of a wing of his house, Le Manoir, was used as a chapel dedicated to Ste Marie; this was sometimes referred to as a temple. It was not until 1820 that the church of St Peter was

St Peter's Church, Sark, built in 1820

DIAGRAM OF SEATING IN ST. PETER'S CHURCH, SARK

```
         VESTRY              PORCH            VESTRY

         PUBLIC                               PUBLIC
          PEWS                                 PEWS

Prisoner's
  Pew
La Moserie    36 | 27 L'Ecluse        | La Genetière   18 | 9 La Hèche
La Ville                                                  |
Roussel       35 | 26 La Forge        | Aval du Creux  17 | 8 Fregondée
Le Grand                              |                   | 7 La Rue
Fort          34 | 25 La Vauroque     | Port à la Jument 16|
Le Clos de                            |                   | La Ville Roussel
la Ville      33 | 24 Le Port         | La Jaspellerie 15 | 6 de Bas
La Vallette                           |                   |
de Haut       32 | 23 Petit Beauregard| La Tour        14 | 5 La Ville Farm
La Seigneurie 31 | 22 La Pipetrie     | Petit Dixcart  13 | 4 La Seigneurie
La Fripponerie 30| 21 Le Grand Dixcart| Pomme de Chien 12 | 3 Le Clos Bourel
La Duvallerie 29 | 20 La Moinerie     | Le Clos de Dixcart 11| 2 La Donellerie
La Sablonnerie 28| 19 Grand Beauregard| La Collenette  10 | 1 La Rondellerie
                     SEIGNEUR'S PEW
```

PEW OWNERS

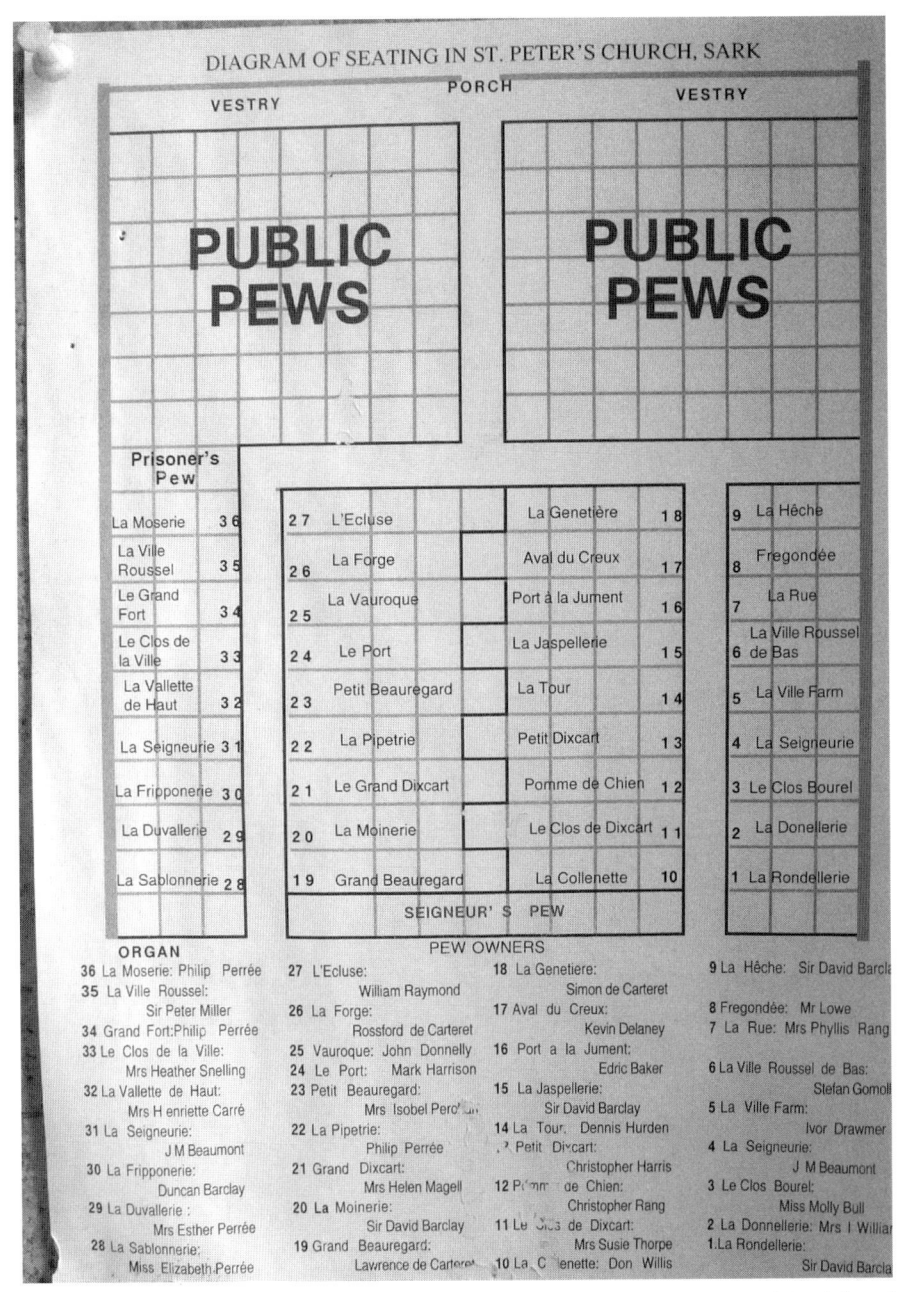

ORGAN
36 La Moserie: Philip Perrée
35 La Ville Roussel:
    Sir Peter Miller
34 Grand Fort: Philip Perrée
33 Le Clos de la Ville:
    Mrs Heather Snelling
32 La Vallette de Haut:
    Mrs Henriette Carré
31 La Seigneurie:
    J M Beaumont
30 La Fripponerie:
    Duncan Barclay
29 La Duvallerie:
    Mrs Esther Perrée
28 La Sablonnerie:
    Miss Elizabeth Perrée

27 L'Ecluse:
    William Raymond
26 La Forge:
    Rossford de Carteret
25 Vauroque: John Donnelly
24 Le Port: Mark Harrison
23 Petit Beauregard:
    Mrs Isobel Perc...
22 La Pipetrie:
    Philip Perrée
21 Grand Dixcart:
    Mrs Helen Magell
20 La Moinerie:
    Sir David Barclay
19 Grand Beauregard:
    Lawrence de Carteret

18 La Genetiere:
    Simon de Carteret
17 Aval du Creux:
    Kevin Delaney
16 Port a la Jument:
    Edric Baker
15 La Jaspellerie:
    Sir David Barclay
14 La Tour: Dennis Hurden
13 Petit Dixcart:
    Christopher Harris
12 P... de Chien:
    Christopher Rang
11 Le ... de Dixcart:
    Mrs Susie Thorpe
10 La C...enette: Don Willis

9 La Hèche: Sir David Barcl...
8 Fregondée: Mr Lowe
7 La Rue: Mrs Phyllis Rang...
6 La Ville Roussel de Bas:
    Stefan Gomol...
5 La Ville Farm:
    Ivor Drawmer
4 La Seigneurie:
    J M Beaumont
3 Le Clos Bourel:
    Miss Molly Bull
2 La Donnellerie: Mrs I Willia...
1. La Rondellerie:
    Sir David Barcl...

A list of the pew owners in St Peter's Church, Sark. The pews are owned in right of property ownership.

built near to the Avenue on land donated by the then *Seigneur*, Pierre Le Pelley. In 1934 Sark became a vicariate.

There is a list of the owners of the church pews in the entrance to the church. The sale of pews in 1820 to the tenements raised the money for the building of the church and the rents go towards its maintenance.

Although the registers of baptisms, burials and marriages date from 1570, several years are missing, as noted. The first register of baptisms, marriages and deaths began on 19 May 1570 and covered through to 1605, but records for 1577–88 are missing. The next register continues until 1757, but with gaps for baptisms 1633–38 and 1664–74 and marriages 1644–61. The third register contains entries for 1675–1702. From 1702 to 1795 there are incomplete records of baptisms and marriages for 1757–95 and no burials are recorded for that period either. The next register opened in 1795 and contains records up to 1820, but also includes some entries for 1787–92 omitted from the previous register.

The new minister in 1795, Reverend Pierre Paul Secretan from Lausanne, Switzerland, sharply criticised his predecessors for the unsatisfactory manner in which they had kept the registers; thereafter the books are reasonably complete until the present day. The registers are held by the vicar. Apart from the omissions recorded above, short gaps also occur at changes of minister.

The Priaulx Library in St Peter Port has two microfilms of the parish registers from 1570 to 1795 and from 1795 to 1899. The Reverend G.E. Lee made copies and these are also available in hard copy. Duplicate Sark church registers (1570–1795) can also be consulted at the Island Archives in St Peter Port, if you are visiting, but they would prefer that postal research enquiries are directed to the Priaulx Library.

The records from 1900 to 1960 are held at the church, although a transcript of them is also held in the archive of La Société Sercquaise. Later entries are in the current books that are still in use at the church.

Smallpox came to the island in 1695, 1705 and 1731, causing the deaths to exceed the baptisms.

Methodism was introduced to the islanders in 1789 when the missionary, Jean de Quetteville, from Jersey, preached in a kitchen; a site was offered and in 1796 the Ebenezer Chapel was built at La Ville Roussel. In the 1920s the new tenant of Ville Roussel gave land for a new chapel which was built adjacent to the old cemetery, and the old Ebenezer Chapel was demolished in 1924. The Priaulx Library in St Peter Port, Guernsey, has copies of these baptisms from 1903 to 2004. Elizabeth Fry, on a visit to the island in 1833, noted that 'in the small island of Sark, with about five hundred inhabitants, they are quite divided religiously, about half of them Methodists, and half members of the Church of England. They will hardly speak to each other.'

In the twentieth century the Roman Catholics on the island have used St Peter's Church for their services. The Priaulx Library has a copy of these baptisms from 1957 to 1991.

In the mid-nineteenth century there was a small Plymouth Brethren assembly; the most notable member being the classicist, William Kelly (1821–1906), who was then the tutor to the *Seigneur*'s children.

Surnames

The names of the forty families who settled in Sark in 1563 are fully covered in *The Fief of Sark*, the definitive book on Sark written by Alfred Ewen and Allan de Carteret. Not only does it give an excellent summary of the history of the island, but it contains invaluable information on the forty families and their descendants and later tenants. Their research notes and working genealogies have been deposited with La Société Sercquaise and give much more detailed information.

Although many of the families came from Jersey, with surnames such as Hamon, Guille and Vaudin, there were others from Guernsey (the Gosselins) and there were also some Englishmen such as William Smith and Robert Slowley. From France there was Regny Le Quedy and from Holland, Jean Hue. Of the forty, quite a few did not stay there long, while others did not leave descendants in Sark (including Helier de Carteret – however, as his nephew did stay on, one can trace back through him to Helier's grandfather and so rejoin the St Ouen line there). It has been said that if you have one single Sark grandparent, then you are related to everyone else with at least one Sark grandparent.

Cemeteries

A medieval cemetery lay to the north-east of Le Manoir, although there is nothing to mark the site now. The first colonists buried there would not have had gravestones. The next cemetery was used from about 1604; it lies to the south-west of La Seigneurie and is adjacent to the Methodist Chapel. A new cemetery was opened in 1855 and surrounds the Church of St Peter. La Société Sercquaise has a transcript of monumental inscriptions and has photographs and a plan of the layout.

Many Sarkese were drowned and their bodies never recovered, so there may be no grave. One exception, for example: on 25 September 1631, returning from Jersey, fifteen Sark inhabitants were drowned and some of the bodies, which were washed ashore in Normandy, were buried there in Carteret. The journey from Sark to Guernsey (or elsewhere) could be a perilous one; in 1839, the then *Seigneur*, Pierre Le Pelley, was drowned with two others. His monument in the church says: *la mer rendra ses morts* (the sea returns its dead). On the east coast there is a large granite memorial to Mr Jeremiah Pilcher, who was drowned with several Guernsey companions in 1868.

The Sark war memorial is situated in front of the church of St Peter. Sadly, during the First World War seventeen men who had joined the Royal Guernsey Light Infantry were killed, most of them in the same incident. They included four members of the Guille family.

Chapter 24

PROPERTY AND OFFICIAL RECORDS

The landholdings of Sark are held by the forty tenants representing the parcels of the forty families who colonised Sark. As explained on the Sark government (website: www.gov.sark.gg): 'There is no true freehold, all land being held on perpetual lease (fief) from the Seigneur, and the 40 properties (Tenements) into which the Island is divided (as well as a few other holdings in perpetual fief) can only pass by strict rules of inheritance or by sale.' The *Seigneur* received a *treizième* (a thirteenth part) of all sales and permission to purchase or sell was originally needed from the *Seigneur*, but this has recently changed to a property transfer tax paid to the island.

La Fripponerie, Sark. First held as a tenement by Julian de Carteret. The curious name suggests mischief or trickery. Although much altered and extended it is now an inn.

The records of all land contracts from 1675 to the present day are complete and available to the public in the Greffe (volumes I–VI, at least). The earliest contract is from 1567 and is of Helier Gosselin's purchase of Beauregard; the original is in the Guernsey Greffe. Most of the other contracts date from 1585 onwards. Many contracts were made or remade in 1612, following King James's Order in Council prohibiting the division of lands. Many were remade in the 1670s to correct illegal sales during the Commonwealth period. As a precaution some tenants had their contracts also registered in the Guernsey Public Registry and a few in the Jersey one.

Inheritance by male primogeniture ceased in 1999 when the Inheritance Law allowed disposal of realty by choice among the children, whether male or female.

The Greffe also acts as a repository for all the records of the Chief Pleas from the same date. The book *The Fief of Sark* by Ewen and de Carteret gives full details of the tenements and their owners; the authors' research notes are kept by La Société Sercquaise. There is a map of the tenements and other properties on: www.sarkelectricity.com/Cadastr/Index.htm.

Divorce has now been possible for Sark residents since 2003 through the Royal Court of Guernsey. Previously couples wishing to divorce had to establish a residency in Guernsey and get a divorce there.

Some of the oldest houses and the windmill (1571) are built in the Jersey style, using pink Jersey granite; later some took on Guernsey features. Many of the new properties created out of the tenements are in a variety of architectural styles. A list of Sark field names is also held by La Société Sercquaise.

In 1941 identity cards for people over 14, most of which have photographs, were issued to all islanders by the German occupying forces and are preserved in the Guernsey Island Archives. They are not filed separately from the Guernsey ones but mixed in with them alphabetically. Children are named on the back of their parents' card.

There are some Sark wills in the Guernsey Greffe; others are in The National Archives, which means that the deceased owned property or assets held in England. These wills are for Philip de Carteret 1766, Anne Drilliot 1836, Abraham Baker 1844 and Evelyn John Gascoigne 1850. In the England and Wales National Probate Calendar (available in digitised form on www.ancestry.co.uk), which covers 1861–1941, there are eleven wills of Sark residents.

Chapter 25

EDUCATION, EMPLOYMENT AND CRIME

Education

Part of the wing of Helier de Carteret's house, Le Manoir, was used as a schoolroom. The rector, Elie Brévint, was the schoolmaster and he kept a series of notebooks; some extracts from them have been transcribed and are available at both the Priaulx Library in Guernsey and the SJL in Jersey.

In 1829 a new school house was built with the assistance of the National School Society on land to the north of St Peter's Church given by the *Seigneur*. Another school (now the headquarters of La Société Sercquaise) was built for girls in 1841 near to Le Manoir, part of which was accommodation for the schoolmistress and part for the class. There are log books from 1896 to 1939 – including a listing of boys and girls, along with the books they borrowed – which are in the possession of La Société Sercquaise. The boys' and girls' schools became the senior and junior schools respectively. In 2004 a new school was built and children now attend there until the age of 16.

Employment

Like other Channel Islanders most Sarkese were both farmers and fishermen. Until the end of the nineteenth century much of the land was ploughed and wheat and barley were the basic currency. Sheep grazed the poorer western pasture and were sent from there to the Guernsey market. Landless families remained poor, some working as servants; they would scavenge for gulls' eggs and samphire.

In 1673 a contemporary writer said that:

> the grand and almost only Manufacture of our Island being knitting which our People perform with a wonderfull dexterity both for Stockings, Gloves, Caps and Waste-coates, Men Women and Children being brought up to it: so that you may commonly see 30 or 40 of them assembled in a Barn, which you would take for a Conventicle of your sweet singers of Israel, for though all ply their knitting devoutly, yet at the same time they tune their pipes.

The Old Prison, Sark, built in 1856, with two cells

In the eighteenth century the opportunities for privateering were such that it became a large source of the wealth of the island. However, this ended with the peace following Waterloo in 1815. The Sarkese had to turn their hands to anything, including fishing; in 1840 the *Saturday Magazine* commented that 'within doors, multifarious occupations may be seen going on, such as tailoring, hat-making, and the like, for in such a limited community as that of Serk [sic], families must provide themselves, by their own labour, with many articles which would be sold by shop-keepers, in other places.'

Mining for silver provided employment for miners primarily from Cornwall, but their presence in the island would have presented other opportunities for islanders, particularly in the provision of public houses. The barracks on Little Sark were built in about 1840 to house them.

Tourism started in the island from about the 1840s and there are now several hotels and guest houses. Artists and writers, such as William Toplis and Mervyn Peake, settled in the island.

Crime

The prison or lock-up was built to the south of the present St Peter's Church sometime after 1597; a new one was built in 1856 and still serves as a temporary lock-up until the prisoner can be taken to Guernsey to be tried at the Royal Court.

Petty crimes are tried locally and recorded in the Acts of the Royal Court. More serious cases go to Guernsey's Royal Court, as do appeals. These records are, therefore, included in those for Guernsey.

Chapter 26

MILITARY AND MIGRATION

Although there was an initial militia, with each of the forty tenants being obliged to carry a musket, by 1744 all men between 16 and 60 had to serve in the militia and keep watch against invasion – through this the militia grew to a force of about 100 men.

The Sark militia was listed in 1805 as a light infantry unit and in 1831 was honoured, along with the other Channel Islands militias, with the designation of 'Royal'. At this time the uniforms were changed from red with yellow facings to red with blue facings and silver lace. After 1881 the facings became scarlet laced with gold. The Sark militia band wore a white uniform with scarlet facings.

In 1869 the force consisted of sixty-eight men with a further twenty-three on reserve, forming two companies, one infantry and one artillery. Disbanded in around 1875, the Royal Sark Militia was listed by the War Office until 1900. Records of the militia during the Victorian period are in the Seigneurie Archive kept by La Société Sercquaise; they even include personal observations on the shooting abilities of individuals.

Many men from Sark served overseas with the Royal Guernsey Light Infantry during the First World War and the island experienced the after effects of the devastating loss of life of Sark men during the First World War. Those who did not return are commemorated on the war memorial in front of St Peter's Church. Their graves are also recorded on the Commonwealth Graves Commission website: www.cwgc.org/, which records graves abroad as well as in Sark.

During the English Civil War Parliamentary soldiers were billeted in Sark, when the island was governed jointly by Captain Nicholas Ling and Judge Jean Le Gros.

In 1793 cannon were sent to Sark from Guernsey to be mounted on the headlands, the island granary was made into an arsenal and a handful of invalid artillerymen came over to supervise the guns. One of the artillerymen, Joseph Hazelhurst, who came to the island before 1805 married twice, had children who married into local families and is buried with a splendid tombstone. His widow started a hotel at Dixcart House, which is still a hotel.

There are a number of fortifications in the island, but much fewer than in the other Channel Islands, probably because of the steep cliffs, which protect the island to a certain extent. Huguenots were encouraged to come to the island, as well as English settlers with the first wave of settlers led by Helier de Carteret.

The Germans occupied the island from July 1940 to 9 May 1945, and two settled in the island, marrying local girls. La Société Sercquaise has lists of German soldiers that were stationed in Sark, as well as the prisoners of war who worked there after the war.

Sark mariners and privateers particularly had contacts with London and some baptisms and marriages of Sarkese are recorded in the French chapel at Wapping. These records are in the collection of the Huguenot Society (see www.huguenotsociety.org.uk).

Many Sarkese have left the island over the centuries. Strays turn up in all the other Channel Islands, especially Guernsey and Jersey (in the parishes of St Peter Port, Guernsey, and St John, Jersey, in particular).

Most of the Cornish silver miners left for America in the late 1840s, although the Remfrey family stayed.

Tourism has flourished since the end of the Second World War, with several hotels, campsites and pubs being established. Many of the workers come just for the season, but inevitably a few remain. With the growth of the European Union, Sark's population has become increasingly cosmopolitan.

USEFUL LOCAL RECORDS AND PRIVATE ARCHIVES

Jersey

Newspapers and Periodicals

The earliest newspaper in Jersey was the *Magasin de L'Île de Jersey* published in 1784 by Mathieu Alexandre. It ceased publication shortly afterwards following a libel suit, but, undaunted, Alexandre started again with the *Gazette de L'Île de Jersey* in 1786; this survived for nearly fifty years, and was followed by a veritable plethora of newspapers that were weekly, bi-weekly or monthly. Most were very partisan, reflecting the political scene of the day by supporting either the Rose or the Laurel Party. There were approximately 100 titles, some of which lasted for only a short time, whilst others changed their name or amalgamated. Now only the *Jersey Evening Post* remains. The newspapers were published in French or English; for example, in 1835 there were eleven papers to choose from, six in French and five in English. The first daily newspaper, the *Jersey Independent and Daily Telegraph*, was published in 1858. For the genealogist the newspapers are obviously extremely interesting and useful for filling in the background detail, though, of course they may not be as accurate as one might wish.

Unfortunately they are not indexed and a great deal of time and patience is required. Apart from specific events they also include information on local births, marriages and deaths, deaths of Jersey people abroad and information on shipping, sometimes with passenger lists. Descriptions of weddings often mention, for example, the bridesmaids and the clothes worn. Sometimes there are accounts of funerals that give lists of the mourners, many of whom were relatives. Obituaries can be enormously helpful, but are not comprehensive. There have been several magazines, such as the *Islander*, which describe social events in the island. There are also numerous smaller publications; of particular interest to the family historian are the church magazines.

Almanacs and Directories

The earliest almanac was published by the same Mathieu Alexandre, of newspaper fame, in 1785. At least thirty-six titles are known to have been

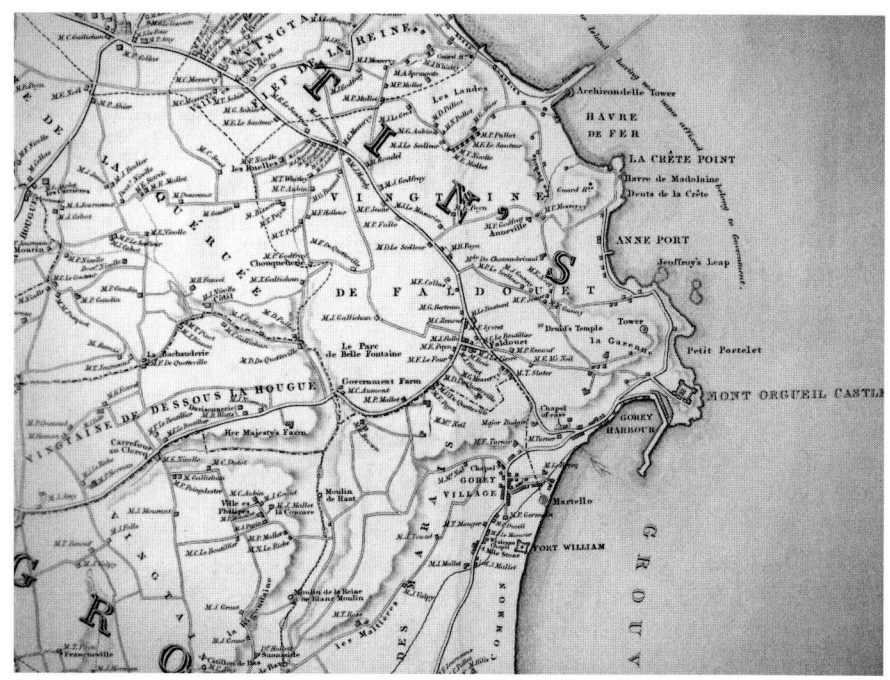

Part of the Godfray map of Jersey 1849, showing Mont Orgueil Castle and houses in the parishes of St Martin and Grouville, with the names of their owners

published since that date. The first English almanac appeared in 1832 and was entitled the *Englishman's Almanac*; it is particularly valuable as it contains a commercial directory for St Helier. After 1849 the almanacs started to list the names and addresses of local residents, and give occupations; before that date details of shipping and the names of local officials were some of the details included. Ships, sea captains and shipping companies are listed, sometimes showing the company flag. As a rule of thumb, the earlier the edition, the less information it contains.

The only directory still published is the *Jersey Evening Post Almanac*, which started in 1911 and in 1937 amalgamated with the *Express Commercial Almanac and Directory*. From the 1880s the almanacs include a yearly summary of events, which is much quicker than going through the newspapers. Sometimes maps are included.

The major collections of newspapers and almanacs are held by the Jersey Library and the SJL; their collections overlap in some areas, but each contains unique items, so, for a thorough search both libraries should be used. The major runs are: (in French) *Almanac de Jersey* 1788–1839, *Almanac Historique* 1790–94, *L'Almanac de la Chronique de Jersey* 1814–1950, *Almanac de la Nouvelle Chronique* 1876–1917 (then merged with *La Chronique de Jersey*); (in English) the *British Press and Jersey Times Almanac* 1862–1910 (which became the *Royal*

Almanac 1911–13), the *Jersey Express Almanac* 1866–1936 and the *Jersey Evening Post Almanac* 1914–74. They are also available at the SJL and the Jersey Library reference section and the Jersey Archive from 1864 to 1997.

Rating lists and electoral lists are available in the SJL, the Jersey Library and the Jersey Archive. The rating lists that survive mainly date from the eighteenth century, although there are earlier ones. Voting was not confidential in the nineteenth century, so the lists in the newspapers detail the votes cast. Later lists give the names of those eligible to vote; women gained the vote in 1919 but the ballot is now secret.

Maps

There are two maps that are particularly helpful to a family historian in Jersey. The Godfray map of 1849 shows most of the houses in the country parishes with the names of their owners. There is an index of house owners at www.rootsweb.ancestry.com/~jfuller/ci/1849map/intro.html.

The Duke of Richmond map of 1787 (engraved in 1795) also shows houses and other buildings, but no names are given. Both these maps have been recently reprinted and can be purchased from the Société Jersiaise. A recent publication that may also be useful is *Jersey Place Names*: published in two volumes, one is a dictionary of place names and the other a detailed map of the island.

Private Archives

Both the SJL and the Jersey Archive have collections of private archives; these range from legal documents, letters and diaries to photographs and ephemera. Even if they do not relate to your particular family, it can be helpful to read some to get a feel for life in the islands.

Guernsey, Alderney and Sark

Newspapers, Periodicals, Almanacs, Directories and Maps

The Priaulx Library has a large collection of local newspapers dating from 1791 when *La Gazette de L'Î Ile de Guernesey* was published. These newspapers would give news from England, Europe and abroad and often the papers would mention news from the other islands, including Jersey. Advertisements are very useful for details of house sales, schools, dentists offering services, and sales of goods, such as cod or Indian shawls.

The early newspapers are in French and it was not until 1813 that the *Guernsey Star* was published, in English. The *Star* has been digitised for the years 1819–48 and is searchable. The Guernsey newspapers include news from all the islands in the Bailiwick. Altogether a total of twenty-four newspapers are known to have been published, fourteen of which were in

English, though some only lasted a few years. Today there is only one newspaper, the *Guernsey Press and Star* (see: www.thisisguernsey.com, which has photos that can be ordered).

Newspapers often included family notices, but these have not been indexed. If the date is known, it is worth checking, as extra information can be included, such as names of bridesmaids and sometimes what the bride wore at weddings, or in funeral notices mourners are given.

There are many maps of Guernsey and the other islands, but most were drawn for navigational purposes. In 1787 William Gardner surveyed the island and his map of Guernsey showed all the houses at that date. The map is reproduced in *Guernsey Houses*, the original is in The National Archives, M/1/1334, and a copy can be purchased from the Guernsey Museum, see: www.museum.guernsey.net.

A book, *Guernsey on the Map*, reproduces many of the maps of the island; there is also a website: www.guernseyonthemap.co.uk.

There is a large collection of almanacs and directories dating from 1791 in the Priaulx Library. Some almanacs are in French, but the later ones are in English.

The Guernsey Museum and Art Gallery collection includes portraits and also has an excellent collection of photos of the island and its people taken by William Frederick Guerin in the late 1800s and early 1900s. For further information see: http://guernseymuseumsgalleries.e-printphoto.co.uk. The collection of almanacs dating from the late 1700s includes Alderney and Sark.

Private Archives

The Priaulx Library and the Island Archives, as well as the Greffe, hold a large number of private documents for many families. These may include, for example, *livres de perchage*, letters or inventories. Some documents may have been used in articles in either the Transactions of La Société Guernesiaise, the *Review of the Guernsey Society* or the journals of the Family History Section of La Société Guernesiaise. Marie de Garis in her article 'St Pierre-du-Bois in the 18th and early 19th centuries', (*Review of the Guernsey Society*, 1949, pp. 479–88) mentions the diary of Jurat Jean Le Mesurier (d.1845), which includes both family information and local happenings.

DIRECTORY OF FAMILY HISTORY SOCIETIES, LIBRARIES AND ARCHIVES

The Channel Islands Family History Society (CIFHS)

PO Box 507, Jersey JE4 5TN
www.jerseyfamilyhistory.org/

This society was founded in 1978, and now has over 800 members from all over the world. Its aims are to encourage research into genealogies and family history of Channel Island families; and to collate and index the contents of the many sources for genealogy. Membership of the society is £15 (single)/£16 (joint) for members living in the British Isles and Europe and £20 (single)/£21 (joint) for elsewhere.

A quarterly journal is published, which contains articles on families, records and methods of research, as well as queries and letters. Upon joining the society members' research interests are printed in the journal, and many members have discovered relatives in this way. A monthly meeting is held in Jersey to which all members and would-be members are invited. In the winter a series of workshops are held to help members with their research.

The society also helps with research for those who are unable to visit the island, and a reduced fee is available for members. The collection of family history material is being added to all the time, and is available to researchers at the Jersey Archive or at the Lord Coutanche Library of the Société Jersiaise.

Journals of the Channel Islands Family History Society start in 1976 and back copies are obtainable from the secretary. The journals are full of interesting articles, including information on records, family trees and lists of strays. The society has several publications for sale, including the indexes for the 1861, 1871 and 1901 censuses.

Jersey

The Société Jersiaise

7 Pier Road, St Helier, Jersey JE2 4XW
Tel: 01534 758314
Fax: 01534 888262
www.societe-jersiaise.org

The Société Jersiaise was founded in 1873 and has a wide interest in all aspects of Jersey life. Its activities cover archaeology, history, archives, geology, natural history, numismatics, bibliography and the study of Jersey Norman French. The Société assists the Jersey Heritage Trust to run the Jersey Museum in Pier Road and it has a museum at La Hougue Bie with archaeological, agricultural and geological displays. The old farm complex, Hamptonne in St Lawrence, has an agricultural museum with activities that show typical Jersey farming.

The Lord Coutanche Library of the society (Société Jersiaise Library – SJL) has an incomparable collection of books, archives and local material of all types. There are many sources for genealogical research, which range from full family trees to notes, and censuses to historical letters. There is a full index of all the genealogical material, which should be consulted before starting research. Notes and family trees compiled by local genealogists– in particular, the Reverend and Madame J.A. Messervy, Charles Langton and Mr A.J. Pepprell – have been deposited here. The bulletin, published annually by the Société, frequently includes articles on local families, and a comprehensive index is in the library.

The censuses for Jersey are available on microfilm, and indexes to them are always being added. The collections in the library also give a great deal of background historical information, which is essential in compiling a full family tree. There are very good collections of local newspapers, almanacs and rating lists.

There is also a large collection of photographs, which is searchable on: www.societe-jersiaise.org/photographic-archive. This includes a large number of portraits taken by Henry Mullins between 1849 and 1873, they include the names of the sitters. In the library there are postcards, maps and prints. There are several newsletters and talks are held throughout the year.

Jersey Archive

Clarence Road, St Helier, Jersey JE2 4JY
Tel: 01534 833300
www.jerseyheritage.org
Email: archives@jerseyheritage.org

Founded in 1993, the archive was opened in a purpose-built building in 2000 and now houses most of the archives of the Lieutenant Governor, the Bailiff and the Royal Court, the States, the parishes and the churches, as well as a lot of private material. Although this book has mentioned many of the records relevant for the family historian, there are many other records, so exploring the archive, either through the website or in person, will be rewarding.

If visiting the archive it is necessary to register by showing photographic identification, and a card will be issued. It is open on Tuesdays, Wednesdays and Thursdays, 9 a.m.–1 p.m. and 2 p.m.–5 p.m. Documents can be pre-ordered by email through the website. Fees are charged for postal, telephone and email enquiries, as well as for photocopying.

The website catalogue is available by going to www.jerseyheritage.org then going to the research centre page and then either to the various pages on research information or directly to the heritage catalogues. If entering a family name in the catalogue, note that a comma is necessary between the surname and Christian name. It is possible to search by names, places, subjects or themes. If the reference is already known that can also be entered.

The Channel Islands Family History Society is based at the Jersey Archive and its collection is on open shelves. A volunteer is on duty to assist with research.

The Superintendent Registrar

10 Royal Square, St Helier, Jersey JE2 4WA.
Tel: 01534 441335
Fax: 01534 441374
Email: marriageenquiries@gov.je
Office hours: 9 a.m.to 12.30 p.m.

If you know the date/name/parish of the event there is a charge of £20 per certificate. If searching is required, a further charge of £10 is levied for a five-year search for a birth or death and £20 for a five-year search for a marriage. Add a postal handling charge of £1 for overseas and 50p for British Isles. Please make cheques payable to 'Treasurer of States'.

For birth, non-Anglican marriage or death certificates that took place in St Helier after 1999, write to:

The Register Office for the Parish of St Helier, 3 Vine Street, St Helier, Jersey JE2 4WB (Tel: 01534 811088, Fax: 01534 811099). The charges are the same as above, but cheques should be made out to 'The Parish of St Helier'.

Adoption

For access to adoption records please write to:
Children's Service, Maison Le Pape, The Parade, St Helier, Jersey JE2 3PU
Tel: 01534 443500

The Jersey Library

Halkett Place, St Helier, Jersey JE2 4WH
www.gov.je/Leisure/Libraries/Pages/index.aspx

The Jersey Library has a good collection of local books, newspapers and almanacs, some of which (mainly newspapers in English) are not available in the SJL. A copy of the indexes to the Superintendent Registrar's books of births, marriages and deaths from 1842 onwards is kept here.

There is also a collection of old telephone directories. The catalogue to the collection is in the reference section, where the staff are very helpful with enquiries. The newspapers and censuses are also available on microfilm. Back copies of *The Times* are also on microfilm. The library has a website with some historical information on it: www.jeron.je/.

The Jersey Society in London

www.jerseysocietyinlondon.org

Founded in 1896 this society encourages those who live outside Jersey to maintain contact. They publish a quarterly bulletin.

The Church of Jesus Christ of the Latter-Day Saints,

St Peter's Valley, Jersey JE3 3DL
Tel: 01534 482171

The church includes a computer room, where they hold microfilm/computer data for all over the world; for example, they have the births, marriages and deaths records for the UK 1837–1983. They allow access to people who are not Mormons to trace relatives. Viewing information is by appointment, but unfortunately the room is temporarily closed.

Guernsey, Herm and Jethou

La Société Guernesiaise (Family History Section)

PO Box 314, St Peter Port, Guernsey GY1 3TG
www.societe.org.gg/sections/familyhistory.php
Email for research enquiries: mariavdt@hotmail.com

The Family History Section has been established since April 1987 and has a current membership of about 250 people worldwide. They have a small research room situated at the Lukis Observatory, in the rear car park of Lukis House, The Grange, St Peter Port, Guernsey, where there is a good collection of archive material.

They have a steadily growing collection of family files and trees compiled and very kindly donated by members and correspondents. The section holds a collection of Guernsey magazine obituaries from 1872 to 1889, which can be very informative, especially if the death took place overseas, and notices of birth, marriage and death entries from 1994 extracted from the *Guernsey Evening Press*.

The indexes are available of the St Peter Port Town Hospital records, 1743 to 1856, and of the St Peter Port Poor Law records for 1811 to 1904.

The journal is published twice a year, as well as two newsletters and there are also regular meetings. Copies are held by the Section and in the Priaulx Library.

The research room is manned by volunteer members, and is open to all members of La Société Guernesiaise by appointment. A small group of

The Lukis Observatory was built in the grounds of Lukis House in the Grange by the Meteorological Office of Guernsey in about 1921. It is now used as the headquarters of the Family History Section of La Société Guernesiaise.

members undertake research on behalf of correspondents; although no charges are made, a donation to assist with costs is appreciated. Over the years, the section has been extremely successful in putting correspondents and members in touch with others researching the same families.

The Transactions of La Société Guernesiaise have been published since 1882; many articles will be of interest to family historians, such as 'Guernsey Pioneers in Australia 1841–1862' by J. Le Pelley, and an index to them is available on: www.societe.org.gg/publications/transactionsindex.html.

The Priaulx Library

Candie Road, St Peter Port, Guernsey GY1 1UG
Tel: 01481 721998
www.priaulxlibrary.co.uk
Email: info@priaulxlibrary.co.uk

Founded in 1889, the library has an excellent collection of books on English local history as well as books on Guernsey, Alderney, Sark, Herm and Jethou as well as Jersey. There is no entrance fee and inter-library loans are possible. There is an online catalogue available on the website. Copies of entries in the parish and civil registers cost £1 per entry.

There is a complete run of the army lists and most of the navy lists and there is a large collection of local newspapers, some of which have been microfilmed. There are many almanacs and directories, the oldest of which is dated 1791. Electoral lists date from 1982.

A large collection of files of family trees that have already been researched by the library staff and other researchers are available. Many documents relating to local families, including letters, are housed here. For overseas enquiries there is a form on the website that gives the terms and conditions and the payment information.

Microfilmed copies of the parish registers are held here, by permission of the rectors; they are for private use and if publication is intended then their permission should be sought. Many of the indexes were created by members of the family history section of La Société Guernesiaise. The index for the wills of personalty, from 1664 to 1899, which are kept by the Ecclesiastical Court, is on microfilm.

There are about 600 maps in the collection, the earliest of which is 1588. The late Carel Thomas, a press photographer, left his collection of photographs to the library and, as many are scanned, it is hoped to put them online shortly. Reproductions can be made. The library also has a large collection of heraldic plaques decorating the bookcases and walls.

The Island Archives

St Barnabas, Cornet Street, St Peter Port, Guernsey GY1 1LF
Tel: 01481 724512
Fax: 01481 715814
Email: archives@gov.gg

For further information see: http://user.itl.net/~glen/archgsy.html (note, however, that some of the information is now out of date). See also: www.bbc.co.uk/guernsey/content/articles/2009/01/19/island_archives_service_feature.shtml.

Visits are by appointment only.

Started in 1986, the Island Archives holds most of the States of Guernsey archives – for example, the town and country hospital journals (which start in 1741) and many records of the Royal Court. There are catalogues available.

All the parochial records have been deposited and these include the strangers' register dating from 1892, and the St Peter Port records of those who were deported from the island.

Records dating from the German Occupation include the identity registration cards, applications for returning evacuees and the property compensation awards. There are also many private collections, which include *livres de perchage* and family letters.

The Greffe

Royal Court House, St Peter Port, Guernsey GY1 2PB
Tel: 01481 725277
Fax: 01481 715097
Email: HMGreffier@gov.gg
Office hours: 9 a.m.–5 p.m.

For family history enquiries please apply to the Priaulx Library in the first instance. For further research apply through the Island Archives. Permission for admission, otherwise, has to be in writing.

The charge is £17 for a full certificate, payable to the States of Guernsey. A search fee of £5 has recently been introduced. If you are in Guernsey, this charge can be avoided as there is public access to the strong room between 2 p.m. and 4 p.m. for a nominal £1 charge and details can be copied from the records.

The records of the Greffe are extensive and have been catalogued (see Island Archives). These include the civil birth, marriage and death records, and all property records, including wills of realty. There are also many manuscripts, maps and plans.

Wills of personalty can be copied at a cost of 30p per page. Permission has to be obtained from the Ecclesiastical Court, but this will be arranged by the Greffe.

Adoption

For information on adoptions from Guernsey, Alderney and Sark:
The Births Records Counsellor, Perruque House, Rue de la Perruque, Castel, Guernsey GY5 7NT
Tel: 01481 256923

The Guernsey Society

www.guernsey-society.org.uk
This society is for all those with an interest in the Bailiwick of Guernsey. The society holds meetings in both London and Guernsey and publishes a review three times a year. There is a complete index to all the articles since 1945 and copies of articles can be sent by email at a cost of £1. There is a page on the website on family history and links to members' family trees.

Alderney

The Family History Researcher

Mrs Eileen Mignot, Maison Tourgis, 8 St Martins, Alderney GY9 3UB

The Alderney Society and Museum

The Museum, High Street, Alderney GY9 3TG
Tel: 01481 823222
www.alderneysociety.org/society.html
email: admin@alderneymuseum.org

The museum staff answer enquiries on all topics, but family history research is usually redirected to Mrs Eileen Mignot, who has copies of all the records.

The museum has a collection of artefacts, documents and photographs and has several exhibition rooms that display the island's history, natural history and geology, and much more. The society has a membership of about 600 and publishes an annual bulletin along with other publications.

Sark

La Société Sercquaise

www.socsercq.sark.gg
The society was founded in 1975 to study, preserve and enhance Sark's natural environment and cultural heritage. The museum is open April to September on Mondays and Wednesdays 11 a.m.–1 p.m., 2 p.m.–4.30 p.m. and Fridays 11 a.m.–1 p.m.

Marie and Richard Axton of the society have indexed all the *seigneural* records, which date from 1580. For family historians there is a growing amount of useful material. There is a library with over 1,000 books and pamphlets on anything to do with Sark, particularly natural history, and there are miscellaneous donations of unpublished papers, such as diaries, theses or works of scholarship (including the working papers of A.H. Ewen, co-author of *The Fief of Sark*, 1969, on the genealogy of Sark families and the inheritance of tenement lands), together with photographs and newspaper cuttings.

The papers of A.H. Ewen include his indexed transcription of the registers of baptisms, marriages and burials, kept by Sark's ministers (1570–1899). There is also a fine study of Sark's tombstones, made by Société members during the 1970s. The Victorian censuses for the Channel Islands and some other historical documents are viewable on CD. There are also family trees for the de Carteret, Hamon, Guille and Drillot families.

From the Second World War there is an important collection of papers relating to the 'friends of Sark' – people who became pen pals to islanders who were interned on the continent and later raised money for post-war reparations – and a documentary record *Sark and Channel Island Deportations* by Tom Remfrey.

Since 2009 the Seigneurie Archive, comprising some 1,500 documents, has been deposited with the Société. These are the working papers of Sark's *seigneurs* from Helier De Carteret, who was granted the island by Elizabeth I back in 1565, right through to the death of Dame Sibyl Hathaway in 1974. They were calendared and catalogued in 1991. Roughly half the documents are deeds for property transactions in Sark and Guernsey. These include the property holdings of the Sark Judge and Guernsey merchant Jean Le Gros (whose daughter Suzanne bought the fief in 1730) and also of the Guernsey privateer John Allaire (whose daughter purchased the fief in 1852).

The other half are miscellaneous, mostly relating to the administration of the *Seigneurie* estate (collection of *rentes* and tithes) and the government of Sark. There are records relating to milling and mining, the Sark militia, the appointment of church ministers and the building of Sark churches and schools. The period 1927–74 is represented by typescript drafts of Dame Sibyl's writings and by copious newspaper clippings of her public appearances to promote Sark in Europe and America.

Channel Island Societies Abroad

New Zealand

> Keith Vautier, 38 College Road, St Johns, Auckland 1072, New Zealand
> email: ChannelIslandsSIG@genealogy.org.nz
> www.keithspages.com/channel.html

Keith Vautier has been appointed the Channel Islands contact for the New Zealand Society of Genealogists (NZSG) and he is happy to answer genealogical enquiries relating to Channel Islands research. He is also available to attend branch research days with the CI collection.

The former Channel Islands Interest Group has placed a wide variety of books, journals, fiche, audio tapes, video tapes, family folders and maps in the NZSG Library. These are available for members to research or to borrow by post within New Zealand. For the list of holdings consult the library catalogue available on this website. Shona Sinclair has a project – collecting Channel Islanders to New Zealand – which is on Keith Vautier's pages. For further information on New Zealand see Olwyn Whitehouse's website: http://freepages.genealogy.rootsweb.ancestry.com/~nzbound/green_dolphin_st.htm.

Gaspé

There are two groups for the Gaspé: the Association Gaspé-Jersey-Guernesey (www.gogaspe.com/gcis/islands.html) and that organised by Jean-Claude Dumaresq, 165-A, rue Renard Est, Gaspé, Québec, Canada G4X 5K9.

For an index of Channel Islanders in the Gaspé see: www.tonylesauteur.com/arbre11.htm.

DIRECTORY OF PLACES OF HISTORIC INTEREST TO VISIT

Jersey

Jersey Heritage

www.jerseyheritage.org/places-to-visit

The Jersey Museum has displays on local history and an art gallery, whilst the Maritime Museum focuses on everything to do with Jersey's great maritime past. The Occupation Tapestry was made by parishioners of each of the twelve parishes to celebrate fifty years of liberation from the German Occupation.

The two castles, the medieval Mont Orgueil and the castle named after Queen Elizabeth I, as well as being fascinating places to explore, have exhibitions. La Hougue Bie is a stunning Neolithic covered-passage grave and Hamptonne is a Museum of Country Life with three farmhouses and a cider orchard.

Guernsey

Guernsey Museum and Art Gallery

Candie Gardens, St Peter Port
Tel: 01481 726518
www.museums.gov.gg

This museum shows the story of Guernsey from the Neolithic to the present day, with particularly good archaeological displays, as well as information on farming and tourism. There are special exhibitions annually. The website has historical information together with photographs and reproductions of paintings, which can be purchased online.

Castle Cornet

St Peter Port
Tel: 01481 721657

The castle was first built after 1204 when King John lost his possessions in Normandy; but the site also has prehistoric origins and was originally cut off from the island. Not only is the history of the castle comprehensively covered, but there is also an excellent maritime museum that displays objects from the Roman ship discovered in St Peter Port harbour. Two other galleries display the stories of the Royal Guernsey Light Infantry, the Royal Guernsey Militia (including many photographs) and 201 RAF Squadron, which is associated with Guernsey.

There are many forts and towers around Guernsey that are worth visiting to get an idea of the enormous amount of fortification which the island has undergone through the centuries, including by the Germans during the Second World War.

The National Trust of Guernsey

www.nationaltrust-gsy.org.gg/

The National Trust owns two properties of particular interest: 26 Cornet Street is probably the earliest remaining complete building within the town's medieval boundaries; this eighteenth-century house has been restored by the trust as a Victorian shop and parlour.

In the parish of Castel the Saumarez Park Folk & Costume Museum has a unique collection of costumes and artefacts consisting of material from within the Bailiwick of Guernsey. It includes men's, women's and children's clothes for all occasions and every accessory imaginable – hats, bags, gloves, shoes, scarves, muffs, tippets, galoshes and spats. There is also a significant collection of civilian and military uniforms, including an example from the Royal Guernsey Militia 3rd (North) Regiment. There are also several rooms showing typical Guernsey interiors and a lot of information on occupations in the island, including an exhibition on the tomato industry.

The Guernsey Tapestry

www.guernseytapestry.org.gg/

This tapestry tells a thousand years of island history in ten panels stitched by residents of each parish to celebrate the millennium; it is housed at the Church of St James in College Street, St Peter Port.

GLOSSARY

The following words are French words commonly used in genealogical records in the Channel Islands. Some words, however, are either unique to Jersey, Guernsey, Alderney or Sark, or unusual in English or French records. In most cases the French and English versions are given. The patois tongues were rarely written and do not appear in official documents.

Lundi	Monday
Mardi	Tuesday
Mercredi	Wednesday
Jeudi	Thursday
Vendredi	Friday
Samedi	Saturday
Dimanche	Sunday
Janvier	January
Février	February
Mars	March
Avril	April
Mai	May
Juin	June
Juillet	July
Août	August
Septembre	September
Octobre	October
Novembre	November
Décembre	December
Baptisé(e)	Baptised
Contrat	Contract
Delaisée	Widow
Demoiselle (Dlle)	Lady
Décès	Death, the late, deceased
Douaire	Dower (widow's life share of husband's estate)
Ecuier	Esquire
Église	Church
Enfant postume	Posthumous child
Enterré/e	Buried
Femme	Wife

Fille (Fe.)	Daughter
Fils/Fille naturel/le	Illegitimate son/daughter
Fils (Fs.)	Son
Gentilhomme (Gent.)	Gentleman
L'ainé	Eldest/elder
Le puiné/Le plus jeune	Younger/youngest
Marraine	Godmother
Maître (Me.)	Mister/Mr
Maîtresse (Mse.)	Mistress/Mrs
Mari	Husband
Marié/e/s	Married
Monsieur (Mr.)/Sieur	Mister/Mr
Né(e) dans la paillardise	Illegitimate child
Né/e	Born
Noces	Marriage
Noyé(e)	Drowned
Parrain	Godfather
Paroisse	Parish
Rât	Parish rate
Ténant	Holder of property feudal term
Testament	Will
Temoin	Witness
Veuf/Veuve	Widower/Widow
Viduté	Widower's inheritance
Abreuvoir	A watering place, mainly for farm animals.
Avocat	Advocate, a lawyer who is both a barrister and a solicitor.
Appariement	A list of a lands held on a certain fief, naming the holders, and stating the services and dues owned by each of them.
Attorney General	Crown officer in Jersey; chief prosecutor.
Bailli, Bailiff	The chief judge in Jersey and Guernsey, and president of the Royal Court and of the States.
Banon	The period between harvest and sowing time when the open fields were proclaimed free as pasture for all the tenants of a fief.
Branchage	Compulsory cutting of trees and overhanging branches by the owner of any land bordering the highway. Carried out twice a year at the present time.
Cabot	A measure of weight; usually used for wheat, but can be used for other items, e.g. apples; one cabot equals approximately forty

	pounds; eight cabots equals one *quarter*. Commonly used in land contracts instead of money.
Canton	Division of a parish in Guernsey; each *canton* is numbered. They replaced the *Vingtaine*.
Centenier	Literally, the man in charge of a hundred households; he is second to the Constable, but senior to *Vingteniers*, who are in charge of twenty households.
Chefs de famille	Heads of family.
Clameur de Haro	Procedure by which a person can stop an alleged wrong being committed on his real property, by calling '*Haro, Haro, a l'aide mon Prince, on me fait tort*' (Haro, Haro, to my aid, my Prince, wrong is being done to me) in the presence of witnesses. This acts as an immediate injunction, and is an ancient right calling for help to Rollo, first Duke of Normandy.
Colombier	A dovecote belonging to the manor house of a fief.
Connétable	Constable, the civic head of the parish who represents it in the States, and presides over the parish assembly. In Jersey he, or she, stands for election every three years and is head of the parish police. In Guernsey there is a senior and junior Constable for each parish, the senior being the head of the *Douzaine*; unlike Jersey Constables, they do not sit in the States.
Contrée	An area of land, usually, in Guernsey, not a measurement. Sometimes used with a family name, e.g. La Contrée Mansell.
Côtil	A steeply sloping field, which is usually cultivated.
Courtil	A small close or field.
Décret/Dégrèvement/Désastre	All terms referring to bankruptcy laws.
Deputé/Deputy	Members of the States in Jersey, first introduced in 1856 – there are now twenty-two, representing all the parishes. Jersey also has Senators who sit on an island-wide mandate. Member of the States in Guernsey and Alderney.

Douzaine	Parish administration in Guernsey, Alderney and Sark. From the French word for twelve. *Douzeniers* are the elected officials.
Extente	List of the Crown's revenues.
Froment	Wheat, frequently used in land contracts.
Governor	Officer appointed to represent the Crown; until 1854 there was a governor, now there is only a Lieutenant Governor, for each Bailiwick, who is appointed for five years.
Greffe	The office of the Royal Court of Jersey and Guernsey or States of Jersey.
Greffier	Clerk or secretary of the Royal Court, the States or a feudal court.
Juré/Justicier/Jurats	Twelve honorary, elected judges, who with the Bailiff form the Royal Court. An ancient post, possibly pre-medieval, they are elected by the Royal Court and the States.
Lavoir	A communal washing place. When served by a stream rather than a spring it is often called a *douet à lavoir*.
Livre de perchage	In Guernsey, these are books that list holders of land in fiefs.
Livres tournois	The legal currency in the islands until October 1834; there was no actual coin or note of this denomination, but it was made up of smaller coins, *sols* and *deniers*: twelve *deniers* made a *sol*, and twenty *sols* made a *livre*. Originally minted in Tours, they were worth less than coins minted in Paris.
Marriage stones	A stone, usually placed over the front door of a house, bearing the initials of the owner; the date may not, however, be the date of the marriage, but may indicate the date of rebuilding. Many of these have been identified, and the information is listed in *Old Jersey Houses*, Vol. II by Joan Stevens. See Alex Glendinning's website (http://members.societe-jersiaise.org/alexgle/stonegsy.html).
Militia	A force of able-bodied natives formed to defend the islands. In 1337 the Jersey militia were reformed. Service was unpaid and compulsory for all able-bodied men from the age of 17 to 65. There were many

	changes over the centuries, but it survived until 1929, when it became a small volunteer force.
Partage	The sharing of an estate of a deceased person among the heirs.
Préciput	The right of the eldest son to the principal share of the real property; this kept farms intact to a certain extent.
Principaux	'Principals' – ratepayers who are assessed above a certain figure, and are therefore entitled to attend the parish assembly, and vote on parish issues. The figure has varied at different times and in different parishes.
Procureur	A person authorised to act on behalf of another person or body. A *Procureur du Bien Publique* is a trustee of parish property. Her Majesty's *Procureur* in Guernsey is one of the Crown officers equivalent to the Attorney General in Jersey.
Rentes	In origin a kind of ground rent payable to the grantor of land by the grantee out of the produce of the land. Even when the notion of absolute ownership of land had developed, a sale of land could be regarded as a perpetual lease, the purchaser paying no cash but agreeing instead to the perpetual payment of an annual *rente* to the vendor and his heirs. An owner of real property could also raise money by creating a *rente* secured on it without parting with the ownership. In this sense it resembles a loan secured on real property. Payment was formerly in kind, usually wheat, and the Royal Court would annually fix the price of wheat which therefore also fixed the price of a *rente*. This was changed in the eighteenth century. An account of *rentes* owed was kept in a *rente* book, or *livre de quittance*.
Seigneur	The lord of a fief, the possession of which entitled certain rights over the land and the persons (*tenants*) living on the fief. All seigneurial rights were abolished in 1966 in Jersey and in 2003 in Guernsey. They have been reduced in Sark in 2008.

Seneschal	A feudal officer. In Sark the *Seneschal* was the chief judge and the president of the Chief Pleas.
Tuteur	A guardian of a fatherless minor; usually the seven nearest relatives form a *tutelle*, which is registered in the Royal Court. The age of majority was 20 in Jersey, since 2000 it has been 18. In Guernsey the age of majority is also 18; this was changed from 20 in 1978.
Usufruit	Usufruct: the use of another's property for a period of time, usually for a lifetime.
Vingtaine	Division of a parish in Jersey (and formerly in Guernsey), which originally referred to twenty households.
Vingteniers	Parish officials representing each *Vingtaine*.
Ville	'Town', but can also be the equivalent of a hamlet with the family name attached, e.g. Ville Machon (Jersey).
Vergée	A local land measurement of approximately 2,150 English square yards. One English acre is equivalent to about two and a quarter *vergées* in Jersey and in Sark, though in Guernsey it is almost two and a half *vergées*.
Vraic	Seaweed: this used to be gathered in large quantities for fertiliser; there were stringent regulations as to when and where it could be cut, and by whom.

SELECT BIBLIOGRAPHY

This selective list includes titles useful to genealogists and family historians, some of which are still in print, but others will only be obtainable at either the British Library in London, the Société Jersiaise and the Jersey Library in Jersey or the Priaulx Library in Guernsey. Inter-library loans are possible. Some titles may also be for sale in second-hand bookshops or through Internet sites. Many older publications have now been digitised and are available on the Internet. Several family histories have been published, but the majority have been published privately. They are not listed below, but can be found in library catalogues.

CHANNEL ISLANDS

Cohen F. and N. du Quesne-Bird, *Silver in the Channel Islands*, Jersey, 1996
Harris, Roger E., *Islanders Deported Part One*, Wiltshire, 1979
Jamieson, A.G. (ed.), *A People of the Sea: The Maritime History of the Channel Islands*, London, 1986
Mayne, Richard, *Old Channel Islands Silver, its Makers and Marks*, Jersey, 1969
McCormack, John, *Channel Island Churches*, Chichester, 1986
Read, Brian Ahier, *No Cause for Panic: Channel Island Refugees 1940–45*, Jersey, 1995
Skidmore, Gil (ed.), *Elizabeth Fry: A Quaker Life: Selected Letters and Writings* New Haven, CT, 2005
Turk, Marion, *The Quiet Adventurers*, Ohio, 1971
— *The Quiet Adventurers in North America*, Ohio, 1975
— *The Quiet Adventurers in Canada*, Ohio, 1979
Williams, Caroline, *From Sail to Steam: Studies in the Nineteenth Century History of the Channel Islands*, Chichester, 2000
Woolmer, Stanley and Charles Arkwright, *Pewter of the Channel Islands*, Edinburgh, 1973

Jersey

Aubin, C.N., *A Glossary for the Historian of Jersey*, Jersey, 1997
Backhurst, Marie-Louise, *Family History in Jersey*, Jersey, 1990
Balleine, G.R., *A Biographical Dictionary of Jersey*, 1948
Bertrand Payne, James, *An Armorial of Jersey*, 1874
Bois F. de L., *The Parish Church of St Saviour, Jersey*, Chichester, 1976

Brett, C.E.B., *Buildings in the Town and Parish of St Helier*, Belfast, 1977
Corbet, Francis, *A Biographical Dictionary of Jersey*, Vol. II, Jersey, 1999
Croad, George W., *A Jersey Album*, Jersey, 1981
Fenn, R.W.D., *'Far Superior to Any Granite Hitherto Found in the Channel Islands': The History of Ronez Quarry, Jersey*, Leicestershire, 2005
Gayler, Michele, *Le Cornu, from Jersey to You: The Story of the First Le Cornu to Come to South Australia, Those who Followed him and Those who Remained Behind in Jersey, Channel Islands*, Adelaide, 2002
Glendinning, Alex, *An Eye on the Past*, Vols 1 and 2, Jersey, 1992 and 1993
— *Did your Ancestors Sign the Jersey Oath of Association Roll of 1696?*, Jersey, 1995
Hampton, Rosemary, *A Jersey Family from Vikings to Victorians*, Jersey, 2009
Jean, John, *Jersey Sailing Ships*, Chichester, 1982
Kelleher, John, *Triumph of the Country: The Rural Community in Nineteenth Century Jersey* Jersey 1994
L'Estourbeillon, R. de, *Les Familles Françaises à Jersey Pendant la Revolution* Nantes 1886
Moore, Diane, *Deo Gratias: A History of the French Catholic Church in Jersey 1790–2007*, Jersey, 2007
Platt, Colin, *A Brief History of Jersey*, Jersey, 2009
Podger, Alex, *Jersey, That Nest of Vypers*, Jersey, 2007
Ronanye, Ian, *'Ours': The Jersey Pals in the First World War*, Gloucestershire, 2009
Steel, Don, *Discovering Your Family History*, London, 1980 (this is based on the Honeycombe family, and includes a chapter on Jersey)
Stevens, Joan, *Old Jersey Houses and Those who Lived in Them 1500–1700)*, Chichester, 1965
— *Old Jersey Houses: From 1700 Onwards*, Vol. II, Chichester, 1977
— *Victorian Voices*, Jersey, 1969
— and Marquerite Syvret (eds), *Balleine's History of Jersey*, Jersey, 1981

Guernsey

Blicq, A.S., *Norman Ten Hundred: A Record of the 1st (Service) Battalion Royal Guernsey Light Infantry*, Guernsey, 1920
Brett, C.E.B., *Buildings in the Town and Parish of St Peter Port*, Belfast, 1975
Crossan, Rose-Marie, *Guernsey 1814–1914: Migration and Modernisation*, Suffolk, 2007
Edwards, G.B., *The Book of Ebenezer Le Page*, London, 1981
Fenn, R.W.D. and A.B. Yeoman, *Quarrying in Guernsey, Alderney and Herm*, Leicestershire, 2008
Garis, Marie de, *St Pierre du Bois: The Story of a Guernsey Parish and its People*, Guernsey, 1996
Glendinning, Alex, *An Eye on the Past in Guernsey*, Jersey, 1993
Goudge, Elizabeth, *Green Dolphin Country*, London, 1944 (novel based on a true story of migration from Guernsey to New Zealand)

Hargetion, Juliette (ed.), *From Our Family Albums*, Vol. 1, Guernsey, 1998
— (ed.) *From Our Family Albums*, Vol. 2 Guernsey, 2002 (Vol. 3 forthcoming)
Hugo, Victor, *Les Travailleurs de la Mer*, Paris, 1876
Ilie, Susan, *Telling Tales: Guernsey News, Views, Ideas, Snippets and Gossip from the Early to Mid-1800s*, Guernsey, 2009
Kreckeler, David, *Guernsey Emigrants to Australia 1828–1899*, Guernsey, 1996
— *The Brothers' Burial Ground 1719–1948*, Guernsey, 2008
Le Poidevin, David, *How to Trace Your Ancestors in Guernsey*, Guernsey, 1987
Le Poidevin, Nick, *Torteval School in Exile*, Jersey, 2010
Marr, L. James, *The History of Guernsey: The Bailiwick's Story*, Guernsey, 2001
— *Guernsey People*, Guernsey, 1984
— *More People in Guernsey's Story*, Guernsey, 1991
McCormack, John, *The Guernsey House*, Chichester, 1980
Monaghan, Jason, *The Story of Guernsey*, Guernsey, 2010
Mosley, David, *Guernsey and the Great War*, Guernsey, 2007
Norman, R.R., *Guernseymen at War: The Royal Guernsey Light Infantry, France and Flanders, 1917–1919*, Guernsey, 2010
Ogier, Daryl, *Reformation and Society in Guernsey*, Suffolk, 1996
Parks, Major Edwin, *The Royal Guernsey Militia (A Short History and List of Officers)*, Guernsey, 1992
— *Dieux Aix: God Help Us – The Guernseymen Who Marched Away 1914–1918*, Guernsey, 1992
Sarre, John W. (compiled), *Guernsey Sailing Ships 1786–1936*, Guernsey, 2007
Schaffer, Mary Ann and Annie Burrows, *The Guernsey Literary and Potato Peel Pie Society*, London, 2008
Stevens Cox, Gregory, *St Peter Port 1680–1830*, Suffolk, 1999
— *The Guernsey Merchants and their World*, Guernsey, 2009

Herm

Kalamis, Catherine, *Hidden Treasures of Herm Island*, Guernsey, 1996
Wood, A.G., *The Channel Island of Herm: An Illustrated History and Guide*, Norwich, 1977
Wood, Jenny, *Herm: Our Island Home*, London, 1972

Jethou

Faed, Susan, *Jethou: Guide and History by the Twenty-Second Tenant*, Guernsey, 1969

Alderney

Brett, C.E.B., *Buildings on the Island of Alderney*, Alderney, 1976
Coysh, Victor, *Alderney*, Guernsey, 1989
Davenport, Trevor, *Alderney's Victorian Forts and Harbour*, Alderney, 2009

Lane Clarke, Louisa, *The Island of Alderney*, Guernsey, 1851
Pancheff, T.X.H., *Alderney Fortress Island*, Chichester, 1981
Venne, Roger and Geoffrey Allez, *Alderney Annals*, Alderney, 1992
Wells, Dorothy H., *The History of the Catholic Church in Alderney*, Alderney, 1994

Sark

Axton, Marie and Richard Axton, *Calendar and Catalogue of Sark Seigneurie Archive 1526–1927*, Vol. 26, London, 1991
Cachemaille, Reverend J.L.V., *Descriptive Sketch of the Island of Sark*, Guernsey, 1875
Carteret, A.R. de, *The Story of Sark*, London, 1956
Coysh, Victor, *Sark: The Last Stronghold of Feudalism*, Guernsey, 1982
Ewen, A.H. and Allan R. de Carteret, *The Fief of Sark*, Guernsey, 1969
Hawkes, Ken, *Sark*, Guernsey, 1992

INDEX

General

America
    American Colonies 15–17, 63, 70, 133
    United States of America 17, 25, 93, 110
    New Jersey 70
Australia 17, 25, 66, 70–1, 108, 111, 134, 162
British Library 12, 24
Canada 17, 25, 70, 98, 108, 110
    Newfoundland 17, 31, 35, 38, 60, 62, 70, 104
    Gaspé 61, 70, 166
Channel Islands Bibliography 12
Channel Islands Family History Society (CIFHS) 4, 7, 24, 29, 32, 43, 97, 157, 159
Channel Islands Mailing List 8
Channel Islands Great War Group 45, 68, 109, 126
Church of Jesus Christ of the Latter Day Saints (Mormons) 8, 40, 49, 50, 51, 70, 160
Cyndi's List 7
England 1–3, 23, 35, 58, 60, 69, 72–3, 80, 85, 93, 102–3, 105, 111
France 1, 22, 58–60, 62, 70, 85, 102, 110, 116, 126, 133, 145
    Army 68
    Brittany 2, 41, 72
    Normandy 1–2, 16, 18, 41, 56, 58, 72, 79, 145
    registration of births, marriages and deaths 23, 85
FreeCen 24
GenForum 8
GENUKI 7
National Archives, The 9, 24, 27, 51, 66–68, 72, 85, 100, 147
New Zealand 17, 25, 71, 111, 165–6, 176
Oxford Dictionary of National Biography 9
Probate Registry, London 51, 100, 147
Rootschat 8
Rootsweb 8
Society of Genealogists 12, 24, 85, 86
South America 70, 105, 108

Alderney

administration: island 1, 4, 116
adoptions 119, 164
agriculture 1, 115–16, 127, 131
Alderney Museum 121, 126, 129–33, 164
Alderney Society, The 129, 132–3, 164
almanacs and directories 12, 155
Archives 127, 164
Army, British 118
    see also garrison
bibliography:
    Internet 12
    select 177–8
Breakwater, The 116–18, 126, 133
Calvinists 1
cemeteries 126
censuses 9, 11, 119–20, 121
Church of England 117, 123–4, 130
civil registration Registrar:
    births, marriages, deaths 119
    cremation 97, 126
crime 131
Donkipedia 8
education 130, 131
employment 117, 121, 131, 133–4
family history researcher/volunteer 119, 122, 125, 164
family trees 122
fortifications 118
Freemasons 106, 131
garrison 125, 127, 132

179

Alderney *(continued)*
geography 2, 115
German Occupation (*see also* World War II) 118, 125, 127, 131
   Organisation Todt 118
Governors 117
history 11, 116
Internet resources 7–9, 11
language (Auriginais) 1
Land Registry 127
maps 2, 127–9, 155
Methodists 124, 125, 132
migration 1, 118, 125–6, 133–4
Militia 132
names 1, 120, 125
newspapers 12, 155, 156
parish registers: baptisms, marriages, burials 122
photographs 133, 164
population 116, 119–20, 127
Presbyterians 125
Priaulx Library, The, Guernsey 119–20, 122, 125
prison 131
privateering 117, 127
Public Registry *see* Land Registry
refugees:
   French Royalists 27
   French Huguenots 125
Roman Catholics 125
Royal Court, The 116, 119, 127, 131
schools 130, 131
shipping 133
smuggling 117
States of Alderney 116
strays 126
surnames *see* names
tourism 4, 118
war memorial 126
wills of personalty and realty 129
World War I 9, 132
World War II 9
   evacuation 118, 120, 121, 133

Guernsey

administration:
   island 1, 4, 77, 78
   parish 77–9
adoptions 85, 108, 164
agriculture 77, 79–80, 103–4, 105, 168
aliens 88–9, 163
almanacs and directories 12, 98, 106, 155
Army, British 109–10, 162
bankruptcy 100
Baptists 95
bibliography:
   Internet 12
   select 175–7
business 106
butchers 105
Cadastre 99, 127
Calvinists 1, 93
cemeteries 96, 110
censuses 9, 86–9, 101, 112
Church of England 90, 100, 106
   pews 93
civil registration 8, 83–5
   births 83, 85, 163
   deaths 84
   Her Majesty's Greffier 83, 163
   overseas, regimental and chaplain returns 85
clergy 106
crime 87, 92, 108
criminal assizes 101
datestones 98
divorce 100
Donkipedia 8
dower 93
Ecclesiastical Court 100, 129, 162, 163
education 80, 102, 103, 110
   school log books 103
   university 102
electoral lists 101
employment 1, 103–8, 168
English Civil War 80
family trees 3, 8, 160, 162, 164
feudalism and fiefs 79, 99, 101
fishing 103
Freemasons 106
garrison 96–7, 110
   register 91
geography 1, 2, 77
German Occupation (see also World War II) 80, 83, 106, 163, 168
godparents 93, 97

Guernsey Museum and Art Gallery 156, 167
Guernsey Press and Star, The 10, 155
Guernsey Society, The 8, 97, 105, 164
heraldry 162
history 79–80, 167, 168
hospital:
    town 107, 161, 163
    country 107, 163
identity cards *see* registration cards
Independents 95
insurance records 100
Internet resources 7–10
Island Archives 11, 63, 85, 87, 97, 99–101, 106, 108, 112, 163
knitting 1, 104
language (DGèrnésiais) 1
Livres de Perchage 99, 101
maps 2, 99, 155, 156, 162
marriage: (see also civil registration and parish registers)
    majority, age of 101
    contracts 98
    deceased wife's sister 83
Lord Hardwicke's Act 93
Methodists 91, 95
migration 1, 83, 108, 110–12
Militia 109
monumental inscriptions 97
names:
    Christian 1, 97
    surnames 97
National Trust for Guernsey, The 105, 168
Navy, Royal 109, 110, 162
newspapers 12, 155–6, 161–2
parish registers 90–3
    baptisms, 90
    marriages, 90–3
    burials 90, 93, 162
photographs 156
Plymouth Brethren 96
Police 78, 105, 108
population 78, 86, 91
poverty 89, 106–8
Priaulx Library, The 10, 11, 83, 85–7, 90, 91, 94–9, 98–9, 100–2, 106, 155, 162, 175
prison 108

privateering 80, 104
property (Public Registry) *see also* Cadastre 98, 147
Quakers 95
quarrying 80, 86, 94, 105
rates 78, 100
registration cards (German Occupation) 87, 163
refugees:
    French Royalists and clergy 93–4
    French Huguenots 80, 111
    political 111
Roman Catholics 93–4, 103
Royal Court 8, 78, 98, 100
St Peter Port 3, 80, 111, 168
Salvation Army 110
schools *see* education
shipbuilding 104–5
shipping 88, 104
smuggling 80, 104
Société Guernsiaise, La, Family History Section 86–7, 90, 96, 160–2
States of Guernsey:
    members 78
    records 100
stillbirths 85
strays 97
telephone directories 10
tourism 4, 80, 105
war memorials 97
wills:
    personalty 8, 100, 162–3
    realty 99
World War I 9, 109, 168
World War II 9, 80, 85, 110, 168
    evacuation 80, 85, 111
    deportation 80, 111

Herm

bibliography 12, 177
general 3, 4, 10, 81, 86–7
history 81
Internet resources 7–10
map 2
population 86

Jersey

administration:
    island 1, 4, 15, 63, 158
    parish 53
adoption 23, 159
agriculture 1, 17, 60–1
aliens 73
almanacs and directories 12, 46, 66, 153–4
Army, British 67–9, 72
bankruptcy (*décrets*) 49, 53
Baptists 22
bibliography:
    Internet 12
    select 175–6
Bible Christians 40
bigamy 53
businesses 65
Calvinists 1, 17, 30, 37, 41, 71
cemeteries 42
    Superintendent St Helier cemeteries 43
censuses 9, 24–7, 73, 158, 160
Chamber of Commerce 63
Church of England 15, 22, 28–37
church pews 37
Church of Scotland 22, 40
civil registration:
    Superintendent Registrar 19–23, 34, 159
    births 21
    deaths 21, 23
    deaths at sea 23
    marriages 21
    overseas/chaplain/regimental returns 23
    war deaths 69
cod fishing 17, 60–1
confirmation 33
cremation 43
crime 56
criminal assizes 66
datestones 46, 47
divorce 55
dower (*douaire*) 46
Ecclesiastical Court 30, 32, 33, 50, 54–5, 57
education 57
    schools 44, 57–60
    school log books 58–9
    university 57
electoral lists 10, 54
Elim Pentecostal 40
employment 21, 31, 33, 60–6, 72
English Civil War 61
family trees 1, 7, 8, 18, 72, 158
feudalism:
    fiefs 35, 47, 56
    records: *appairements*, *Extentes* 56
fishing 60
Freemasons 65
funeral directors 36, 44
garrison 43, 63–5, 68–9, 72
    register 30
geography 2, 15
German Occupation 18, 25, 43, 50, 55, 59, 167
    evacuation 25, 55, 59
    deportation 55
    Organisation Todt 43, 55
godparents 31
halbardiers 66
heraldry 18
history 1, 16–18
hospital (Hôpital Général) 30, 33, 51, 53, 59, 65
illegitimacy 21, 32–3, 54
Independents 22, 39, 43, 44
inquests 54
insurance records 51
Internet resources 7–10
Jehovah's Witnesses 40
Jerripedia 8
Jersey Archive 10, 19, 28, 29, 38, 44, 47, 48, 49, 52, 53, 59, 60, 63, 65–7, 73, 155, 158
Jersey Evening Post 10
Jersey Heritage 167
Jersey Library 19, 46, 154–5, 160
Jersey Merchant Seamen's Benefit Society 35, 62
Jersey Society in London, The 160
Jews 22
knitting 1, 60, 160
language (Jèrriais) 1, 18, 59
maps 2, 52, 154–5

marriage 3, 34, 35
    age 34
    banns 34
    breach of promise 54
    contracts 49
    eloping 35
    licences 34
    Lord Hardwicke's Law 35
    òu marier (where married) 21
Methodists 17, 22, 38–40, 43–4, 66
migration 1, 25, 69–73
Militia 25–6, 67
monumental inscriptions 42, 44
names:
    Christian 1, 24, 30, 41–2
    surname 40–1, 159
Navy, Royal 67, 72–3
newspapers 12, 53, 153–4, 160
Oath of Association Roll 27
orphans 59
parish registers 28–37
    baptisms 21, 29–33
    marriages 29, 33–5
    burials 29, 35–7, 44
photographs 7, 45, 52, 66, 158
police:
    States 54, 64
    honorary 54, 64
population 15 –6, 30, 42
poverty 33, 54–5, 65
powers of attorney (*procurations*) 50
Presbyterians 39
prison 66
prisoners 61, 66
prisoners of war 62, 68
privateering 61
prostitution 63
Public Registry (*Registre Public*) 8, 46–50, 147
Quakers 22, 40, 42
rates 54
refugees 43
    French Royalists and clergy 27, 37, 58, 71–2
    French Huguenots 17, 71
    Hungarians, Polish, Italian, Spanish 43, 73
registration cards (identity cards) 10, 25

Roman Catholics 22, 37–8, 43–4, 58–9, 66, 72, 73
Royal Court, The 15, 35–6, 50, 52, 63, 159
Salvation Army, The 40
séparation 49
shipbuilding 60, 62–3
shipping 60, 62–3, 69, 73
silversmiths 64
smuggling 17, 61, 63
Société Jersiaise, Lord Coutanche Library (SJL) 10, 19, 40, 44, 47, 48, 50, 59, 61–2, 64, 69, 70–1, 154–5, 158
States of Jersey:
    members 15
    records 53, 159
strays 32
stillbirths 23, 32
suicide 36
Swedenborgians 40
telephone directories 10, 160
tourism 4, 17–8, 64
war memorials 44, 45
wills:
    personalty 50
    realty 8, 50–1
witchcraft 52
World War I 43, 45, 68–9, 73
World War II 18, 22, 25, 43, 45, 73

Jethou

general 1, 3, 4, 10, 81–2, 86, 97, 160, 177
history 81–2
Internet resources 7–10

Sark

administration 1, 4, 11, 138, 140
agriculture 138, 148
almanacs and directories 12, 155
Archives 165
bibliography:
    Internet 12
    select 178
Brecqhou 137–8, 141
Calvinists 1, 140
cemeteries 145
censuses 9, 141, 165

Sark *(continued)*
Church of England 142
  pews 143
civil registration: registrar, births, marriages, deaths 141, 144–5
cremation 97, 141
crime 150
divorce 147
Donkipedia 8
education 137, 139, 148
employment 148–9
English Civil War 151
family trees 165
fief 139–40, 142, 146, 165
fishing 148
French Huguenots 152
geography 1, 2, 137
German Occupation 140
Greffe, The 141, 147
history 1, 138–40, 151
Internet resources 7–9, 11
knitting 148
language (Sercquais) 1
maps 147, 155
Methodists 144–5
migration 152
Militia 151
mill 138

monumental inscriptions 165
names, surname 145
newspapers 12, 155
parish registers: baptisms, marriages, burials 144, 165
Plymouth Brethren 144
police 139
population 139, 141
Priaulx Library, Guernsey 141, 144, 148, 155
prison 149
prisoners of war 152
privateering 149, 152
property 140, 143, 146–7
registration cards (identity cards) 87, 147
Roman Catholics 144
Royal Court 138
schools 137, 139, 148
silver 149, 152
Société Sercquaise 11, 144, 145, 147, 148, 151, 164
strays 152
tourism 4, 140, 149, 151–2
war memorials 145
wills: personalty and realty 147
World War I 9, 145, 151
World War II 9, 152, 165